Larry L. Rasmussen

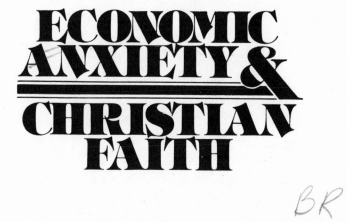

ECONOMIC ANXIETY & CHRISTIAN FAITH

AUGSBURG Publishing House • Minneapolis

ECONOMIC ANXIETY AND CHRISTIAN FAITH

Copyright © 1981 Augsburg Publishing House

Library of Congress Catalog Card No. 80-67795

International Standard Book No. 0-8066-1857-4

Scripture quotations unless otherwise noted are from the Revised Standard Version of the Bible, copyright 1946, 1952, and 1971 by the Division of Christian Education of the National Council of Churches.

NEB refers to The New English Bible, © the Delegates of the Oxford University Press and the Syndics of the Cambridge University Press, 1961, 1970.

Manufactured in the United States of America

contents

To Holden Village

preface

Few things trouble so many people these days as the prospects for economic life. Yet, curiously, there are relatively few materials which address our worrisome economy from the perspective of Christian faith. This book attempts to do that.

The study rests on three assumptions. It is important that they be shared at the outset, since they shape what follows:

1. Something of great significance in our collective economic life is occurring; it has local, national, and international dimensions; and we need to do our best to comprehend it.

2. Economic life affects both body and spirit in many ways, directly and indirectly.

3. Christian faith addresses both body and spirit and has resources for viewing and shaping economic life.

Even a slender volume is never the work of the author alone. I have had generous help from several quarters. A shorter, somewhat different version of this study was published by the Division for Life and Mission in the Congre-

gation, The American Lutheran Church. Charles P. Lutz
invited that writing and offered encouragement and edi-
torial assistance. Time to undertake this project came
through a sabbatical leave from Wesley Theological Seminary. The funds to do so were made available by the
seminary, the Lutheran World Federation Scholarship and
Exchange Program, and a Walsh-Price Fellowship from the
Maryknoll Fathers. The sabbatical year was spent in East
Africa and Central Europe, and leaving the United States
for a time was a lively stimulus for reflecting on American
economic life. While those who made this study possible
cannot be held responsible for the outcome, they have
my gratitude for its realization.

A study project concludes each chapter except the last.
Although the study projects can be undertaken individu-
ally, they are better pursued with others. Since economic
life, like Christian faith, is inherently corporate, we do well
to examine it together.

The dedication to Holden Village is written in admira-
tion. Those of us who stand a long while at the window,
dreaming of what might be, are elated when somewhere
and now and then it comes to pass. I dream of vital Christian communities that connect the faith inherited from
the saints to a joyful economic life shared equitably in
the present and rendered sustainable for future generations. My dream, expressed in the last two chapters of this
book, has already been partially fulfilled in Holden Village.

Larry Rasmussen
Holden Village
Chelan, Washington

1

economic anxiety
and doubt

> The ideas of economists and political phi-
> losophers, both when they are right and
> when they are wrong, are more powerful
> than is commonly understood. Indeed,
> the world is ruled by little else. Practical
> men, who believe themselves to be quite
> exempt from any intellectual influences,
> are usually the slaves of some defunct
> economist.
>
> —John Maynard Keynes
> *The General Theory of Employment,*
> *Interest and Money,* 1936

We have entered a time of great economic anxiety and
doubt. For many, the optimism of the 1950s and the expansiveness of the 1960s is gone. As we enter the 1980s,
the mood is markedly different, more sober. The President of the United States worries aloud about a poll
which records that for the first time a majority of American parents believe their children will not have as prosperous a life as the parents have had. Economists wonder
if the theory that has guided an enormously productive

7

economy is obsolete. Is Lord Keynes himself, the guiding theoretician, now becoming a "defunct economist"?

Is something *fundamentally* wrong? The testimony is disturbing. In the summer of 1979, then Secretary of the Treasury Michael Blumenthal addressed the New York Financial Writers Association:

> As financial and economic writers, you must find this a strange and difficut time. Reliable sources are no longer reliable. Those wonderfully complicated mathematical models of the economy have turned treacherous—they offer as many false leads as correct ones. The experts who know most about the economy now have the least certainty about it. The traditional crystal balls have been reduced to ground glass. Those who are most emphatic in their judgments and prognostications are almost without exception touched with arrogance and blessed with ignorance. Wisdom speaks in terms that are grey, hedged and unquotable.
>
> I can imagine how hard it is to work up a strong lead or a new angle when you sit down at the typewriter. Well, I have no sympathy for you, because I have the exact same problem, when I stand up at a podium like this.
>
> But if you and I have a problem, so do my colleagues, and policymakers and decision-makers, and those who would like to be . . . and those who used to be. These are tough times for all of us.[1]

This is an extraordinary statement for an incumbent Secretary of the Treasury. Its candor lays bare how incomprehensible, how puzzled, economic life has become.

A former Secretary of the Treasury, George Schultz, reluctantly confesses much the same:

> We are in a very unusual period where we more or less cast loose from economic beliefs we once held to be unarguable. We have cast off from a large number of these old moorings, and we have not yet found new ones.[2]

Alfred Kahn, President Carter's "anti-inflation czar," made an amusing remark about economic life in late 1979: "Anybody who isn't schizophrenic these days just isn't thinking clearly."[3]

American consumer behavior and the national mood seem to signal that something is badly out of joint. Americans have usually waited until prices are relatively low and stable before making large purchases (houses, cars, major appliances). But in 1977 and 1978, we said, in effect, "Even though prices are high, the time to buy is now, before prices go yet higher." We also saved less and borrowed more.[4]

What is behind this? A *Time* essayist broods: "There is an unhappy plausibility . . . that Americans have drifted into a condition of spoiled purposelessness."[5]

The *Time* writer anguishes about a people whose lack of direction is matched only by an obsessive pursuit of material indulgence, even when economics would counsel restraint. Yet the essayist is at a loss to explain this behavior.

Perhaps the behavior is a little like that of children on

the playground. When the bell is rung, ending recess, there is a sudden spurt of frantic play. The children quicken the pace to get in one last round. Many Americans may be acting as if they think "time is up" for unbounded affluence as a way of life, but they'll have one last round before teacher ends recess for good. Anxious about the future, they plunge hedonistically into the present, following the logic of Michael Korda advocated in a *Newsweek* column, "Hooray for Hedonism": "The worse things get, the more sensible it is to take what pleasure one can before it's too late." [6]

Or perhaps our economic anxiety and behavior have other causes. Americans have expected economic prosperity to yield happiness. Indeed, "the pursuit of happiness" has come to mean the accumulation of wealth for private enjoyment. But what if the human spirit is not satisfied by growing economic prosperity and technical achievement? What if people depend on improved material well-being to cure their restlessness, and it does not? Then anxiety is heightened when either (1) those expectations of economic life cannot be wrung from it; or (2) economic life is still invested with high expectations but is itself threatened and does not deliver material advance.

Still, this behavior and mood are not really what we mean by economic doubt and anxiety. Three broad, often related, developments have dealt hard blows to the heady confidence of an earlier day. These are:

1. the collapse, in the 1970s, of many of the crucial assumptions of economic policy;

2. the growing gap between rich and poor;

3. slow growth and "limits to growth."

The first we must take up here, the latter two will only be sketched, then treated more fully in later chapters.

CHANGED CIRCUMSTANCES AND COLLAPSED ASSUMPTIONS

Michael Blumenthal, in the address cited earlier, says the big economic story of the 1970s is the shock to the consensus on economic policy which reigned from the '40s through the '60s.

That consensus flowed from the lessons learned in the Great Depression, the effective policies based on the writings of John Maynard Keynes, and the success of government moves in the '60s, chiefly the so-called Kennedy tax cut.[7]

The consensus rested on several assumptions:

1. A steady increase in productive potential was assumed. What economists call "the supply side" of the economy—that which goes into goods and services—would steadily expand. The public management of the economy was to adjust demand for the goods and services produced.[8]

2. It was also assumed that the demand could be manipulated accurately by government to match supply.[9]

3. There would be mistakes, but these could be corrected without great loss to any particular sector of the economy. If demand lagged and caused increased unemployment, government spending or tax cuts would stimulate demand and reduce the number of jobless. If too much demand brought inflationary prices, monetary policies could be tightened to decrease demand.[10]

4. It was assumed that the nation was the major domain for economic policy.[11]

Changing circumstances have challenged all these assumptions, even though we continue to employ them. The supply side of the economy does not take care of itself. It is vulnerable to many things, and what we thought would automatically care for itself now is a matter for close attention. Blumenthal says:

> The nation must now reorient the agenda of economic policy back to basic, supply-side issues—to rebuilding our capital stock, reinvigorating the growth of productivity, creating a new domestic base for the energy needs of the country, and reducing the structural unemployment of human resources that marks every stage of the business cycle.[12]

Not only have the '70s challenged the assumption about the supply side; they also showed that management of the demand side has become extraordinarily difficult. We expected to do "fine-tuning." What we have, instead, in mid-1980, are "the twin ugly evils of accelerating inflation and the long-predicted recession"; [13] and apparently the solutions to one work against the solutions to the other.

Finally, the nation is no longer the major domain of economic policy. The world is. The rise of oil prices in the Middle East, Africa, or Latin America shows up at the pump in every small town in North Dakota or Arkansas. Transnational corporations, even if American-based and largely American-controlled, move their production and marketing forces from one country to another with ease. U.S. monetary policy has not only domestic effects (for example, on buying and selling homes) but influences the value of U.S. currency abroad, which in turn affects the prices of U.S. imports and exports. The worldwide economic linkages are far more complex than U.S. economic policy has assumed.

As a result of these changes, economic life is at a baffling turning point. Blumenthal muses:

A decade or so from now, many of you will no doubt be able to look back and make fine-sounding sense of this period. But right now I think we must all confess to some uncertainty. Many of the old concepts no longer make sense. Yet we are still some distance from having a secure, new intellectual foundation for economic management.[14]

RICH NATIONS AND POOR

In the first decades after World War II there was also a consensus about rich and poor nations: Expanding economies and the benefits of science and technology could put most nations, rich or poor, on the same path to prosperity. Affluent economies were already on that path. Less developed economies were not, but they could be, spurred by the vitality and resourcefulness of the industrialized nations, especially the Western nations led by the United States. President John Kennedy's graphic image gave expression to this confidence. "A rising tide," he said, "lifts all boats."

There was an exuberant optimism, and many shared the outlook of Buckminster Fuller in the 1960s: "Comprehensive physical and economic success for humanity may now be accomplished in one-fourth of a century."

That optimism is now shattered. "Comprehensive physical and economic success for humanity" is not visible in the near future. The picture is perplexing, in part because many of the less developed countries *have* experienced real growth, as predicted. Often, in fact, their rate of growth has exceeded that of the advanced economies. Yet the gap between rich nations and poor has been growing, rather than closing. And increasing inequality, unemployment, and foreign indebtedness have accompanied even the *rising* gross national product of many poor nations.

There is massive human failure here, the failure to narrow the gap between rich and poor when the conditions were of unprecedented prosperity. That failure is one of the major reasons for economic doubt today.

SLOW GROWTH AND "LIMITS TO GROWTH"

One of the unsettling phenomena of the 1970s has been slowed productivity (the output of goods per worker hour). In the U.S. the slowdown has been dramatic. From 1948 to 1955 our average annual growth in productivity was 2.7%; from 1955 to 1965, 2.6%; from 1965-73, 2%. Then for 1973-77 it fell to 0.9%, and for 1978 to 0.8%.[15] 1979 actually saw a negative number for the first time in decades. So productivity has been on the skids.

Scores of reasons are offered. Some are specific: excessive government regulation (forcing spending on items that do not enhance production and often add to costs); outmoded technology and decreased investment in research and development (letting other nations gain a competitive edge); hiring and retaining poorly skilled and low-commitment employees; expanding the economy largely in the service sector, where there is low growth and productivity.

Other reasons are more general. Some contend that the work ethic, which did so much to forge a strong economy, has waned. Others point to a dehumanized work place for many, contending that boredom, once the disease of royalty and the idle rich, is now democratized so that millions suffer from low-level depression and no longer care about work. Or perhaps we have "spoiled purposelessness" that is more attached to consumerism than to productivity.

Quite different reasons for slowed productivity and slowed growth come to the fore in the vigorous debate about "limits to growth." There are several kinds of limits, all interacting in complex ways.

Natural resource limits. The industrial nations' economies have been built on cheap and abundant energy. Energy is no longer cheap, and the end of some vital resources, such as oil, is in sight. Other resources will have to be developed, but that will mean a costly transition period, one for which we are not well prepared.

Environmental limits. There is widespread worry about the "carrying capacity" of a region or the globe as a whole. How many people and other species can be sustained at what level of well-being in a given area? How much heat and carbon dioxide can be released into the atmosphere without disastrous effects for local ecosystems? Or how much waste and pollution? Such questions have recently taken on grave importance as we bump up against the harsh consequences of transgressing environmental limits. They can no longer be ignored without risking an intolerable result. At the same time, the economy is not accustomed to paying, or is not prepared to pay, the heavy costs of environmental maintenance.

Economic limits. Even when potential economic growth is within the limits of available resources and environmental tolerance, economic constraints sometimes impose limits of their own. A current example is that of processing some low-grade ores. Despite technical feasibility, it is not being done because it takes far more energy than processing higher grade ores, and energy is escalating rapidly in price.

The 1970s have seen an interaction of these realities—

resource, environmental, and economic limits. They add up to far more constraints than most Americans experienced in the expansive decades from 1945 to 1965. Some even say that one economic epoch is coming to an end, while another, its shape not yet clear, struggles to be born. Others argue that economic growth can still happen, though without such heavy reliance on certain natural resources, and through expansion in services, the arts, education, and recreation.

But few persons doubt that we are in a time of great economic change and that stakes are high and uncertainties near. The mood is captured well by Ellen Goodman:

> Inside the circumference of our fear of the future is a profound skepticism about the present. We are afraid of seeing the end of the "progressive era." And yet we no longer are convinced that progress is progress anymore.[16]

STUDY PROJECT

1. Were you an economic optimist in the 1960s who became an economic doubter in the 1970s? Can you retrace some of your thinking? How did your present attitudes evolve from your experiences of 10, 15, 20 years ago?

2. How have the three realities—resource, environmental, and economic limits—interacted in your experience? Do you react to these limits with fear and uncertainty, hope, or some other emotion?

3. In an article, "Does Money Buy Happiness?" Richard Easterlin reports the results of a 24-year study on happiness. Periodically from 1946 through 1970 Americans were asked to describe themselves as "very happy," "fairly happy," or "not happy." The replies

given were then correlated with incomes. While from 1946 to 1970 real per-capita income rose 62%, the percentages of "very happy" and "fairly happy" responses did not rise. Two and one-half decades of increased material well-being made little or no change in people's happiness, Easterlin concluded. (Details in Tibor Scitovsky's *The Joyless Economy*, New York: Oxford University Press, 1976.)

What makes *you* happy? Is your answer similar to one you would have given 10 years ago? Would you expect an increase in the happiness of *individuals* whose economic situation went from poverty to middle income? What about those who went from middle income to upper-middle? Do Easterlin's findings fit the general American expectation, the "American Dream"?

2
economics, ethics, and religion

Whenever life denies us the good we had expected, it seems to present us with an alternative good that we did not expect. . . . To stubbornly persist in chasing the expected good at the expense of the offered good would be the greatest possible folly—a folly that the Prophet Isaiah warned about some three millenia ago: "Why do you spend your money for that which is not bread, and your labor for that which does not satisfy? . . . Incline your ear and come to me; hear, that your soul may live" (Isa. 55:2). Sufficient wealth efficiently maintained and allocated, and equitably distributed—not maximum production—is the proper economic aim.

Herman E. Daly
Steady-State Economics, 1977.

Professor Daly is an American economist. But is his paragraph an economic statement, a moral statement, or a religious statement? Reference to "the good" is the language of morality and ethics. "That your soul may live" is a classic religious expression. And the final sentence, "Sufficient wealth efficiently maintained and allocated . . ." is Daly's definition of what economics is—or ought to be.

In the ease with which he moves among all three categories, Daly is not typical of economists in the Anglo-American tradition. Indeed, there has been an effort to keep economics free of encroachments from ethics and religion, despite the fact that capitalism's patron saint, Adam Smith, was a teacher of moral philosophy.

The lines among economics, ethics, and religion have never been clear-cut. Nonetheless, these terms do refer to significantly different realities, and the purpose of this chapter is to differentiate them, while also noting how they overlap in ways we hardly notice.

RELIGION

Religion originally meant "that to which we are bound" or "that which binds us." Religious faith is the network of a person's most binding loyalties, commitments, and convictions. Paul Tillich's term is "ultimate concern." The object of one's ultimate concern is one's final good and one's god, the object of faith. Simply put, a person's religion is that which matters most in life.

Christianity makes a particular religious claim, the claim that God in Christ is the proper object of our most ultimate trust, loyalty, and commitment. Idolatry means to place our ultimate concern somewhere else, to bind our lives elsewhere, to misplace our basic trust.

Martin Luther wrote:

> To have a God is simply to trust and be-
> lieve in one with our whole heart. As I
> have often said, the confidence and faith
> of the heart alone make both God and an
> idol. If your faith and confidence are
> right, then likewise your God is the true
> God. On the other hand, if your confi-
> dence is false, if it is wrong, then you have
> not the true God. For the two, faith and
> God, have inevitable connection. Now, I
> say, whatever your heart clings to and
> confides in, that is really your God.[1]

What one's "heart clings to and confides in" com-
prises one's religion.

Luther goes on to speak of idolatry. He chooses an
example from economic life:

> Many a one thinks he has God and en-
> tire sufficiency if he has money and
> riches; in them he trusts and proudly
> and securely boasts that he cares for no
> one. He surely has a god, called mam-
> mon . . . that is, money and riches . . .
> upon which he fixes his whole heart.
> This is the universal idol upon earth.[2]

ETHICS

Ethics is the offspring of religion. Our notions of what
is good and right (ethics) expresses our most basic convictions and commitments (religion). Our values and
actions exhibit what is most important, binding, or ultimate in our lives.

Christianity makes a particular moral claim, namely,
that God in Christ is the source of the Christian's moral

judgments and actions. Many of these judgments and actions are in the domain of economic life.

ECONOMICS

The tie of economics to ethics is close, though not always apparent. Ethical questions are questions like these: What do we regard as good, and why do we think of it as good? What do we conceive of as the good society, and what values make it so? Why is something better than something else, or worse? Why is one decision right and another wrong? Why is some particular thing more important and something else less so? What is the good life? [3]

Our day-to-day choices and judgments have moral dimensions. This includes our economic choices and judgments. Indeed, one definition of the aim of economics is "how to do the best with what you've got." But what is "the best," if not a moral category, at least in part?

Or recall our opening quotation. "The proper economic aim," Daly says, "is sufficient wealth efficiently maintained and allocated, and equitably distributed—not maximum production." Daly admits that words such as "proper," "sufficient," and "equitably distributed" are value-laden. Behind them rests a notion of "the good society." Indeed, for Daly, economics is in the service of the good society. Economic life is to be organized in keeping with the values that make for the good society.

The point is not whether we agree with Daly's definition of "the proper economic aim." Rather, it is that *any* understanding of the proper economic aim will have moral dimensions. It will have some implicit picture of the good life or the good society. Ethics belongs to life, as does economics, and their respective realities penetrate one another.

THE ECONOMY

"The economy" is that part of a nation's or region's social system which has to do with the production, distribution, and consumption of goods and services. Institutions, resources, processes, labor, regulations, and finance are all involved in this enterprise.

Certain recurring questions are typical for the economy. How are resources, opportunities, and responsibilities fairly apportioned? Who is to receive which benefits and carry which burdens? What is fair compensation for work done? What are the most efficient means of production and distribution? Whose interests are being served by a particular policy or action? How is the common good best served?

If these questions belong to economics, they belong to ethics as well. Words and phrases such as "responsibilities," "benefits," "burdens," "best," "fair compensation," and "the common good" all have moral dimensions.

If we press such words very far, we soon rub up against what matters most to people. That is, we soon rub up against their lived religion. Religion, ethics, and economics all have their complex, but real, ties to one another.

STUDY PROJECT

Only rarely do busy people pause to trace the interplay of their religious loyalties, their moral commitments, their economic choices, and the economic arrangements of their society. Most of the time people accept such matters as "the way things are." That's all the more reason to bring such matters into view, since often the most important things are those an individual or a society considers settled or beyond debate. A time of economic anxiety and doubt creates awareness of these "taken-for-granteds," however, because doubt and anxiety have a way of forcing basic questions. If we can't secure all the energy resources we want, what should we do with those available to us? Where are our priorities? Where ought they be? What kind of society do we want, anyway? What do we want for ourselves and for coming generations? What kind of living pattern is necessary to achieve it? Who should pay what costs?

Some assumptions have governed the lives of many, perhaps most, Americans over decades. These assumptions are in part religious, in that they express basic convictions and beliefs and comprise a kind of "faith" or "creed." They are also moral, in that core values come to expression here. Many are also economic, or have strong effects in economic life. These assumptions are listed below so that readers might begin their own tracing of the interplay of religion, ethics, and economics.

The following might be a useful way of organizing reflection and discussion.

1. Read through the list of cultural assumptions. Then consider the truth or validity of some or all. Are there other major assumptions you would add to the list?

2. Consider the assumptions again, this time with a question in mind: Are any of these assumptions in conflict with the Christian tradition?

3. Choose some current, concrete economic issue and ask, "What are the moral and religious dimensions?" Examples: energy use, food production and distribution, a national health insurance plan, a local bond issue, investment in corporations doing business in South Africa.

4. Discuss whether the word of Jesus that we do not

live "by bread alone" is a moral, a religious, or an economic teaching. What about the petition "Give us this day our daily bread"?

Assumptions Characteristic of American Culture

1. Nature has an infinite storehouse of resources for human use.
2. Humanity has the commission to control nature.
3. Humanity has the right and obligation to use both renewable and nonrenewable resources for continuing improvement in the material standard of living.
4. The most effective way to attain individual and social betterment is through improving the material standards of living.
5. The most effective way to attain higher standards of living is through economic growth.
6. The quality of life is furthered by an economic system directed to ever-expanding material abundance.
7. The future is open; systematic progress for the whole human race is possible; and through the careful use of human powers humanity can make history "turn out right."
8. Modern science and technology have helped achieve a superior civilization in the West.
9. What *can* be scientifically known and technologically done *ought* to be known and done.
10. The good life is one of productive labor and material well-being.
11. Both social progress and individual interest are best served by competitive, achievement-oriented behavior.
12. There is freedom in material abundance; when people *have* more, their freedom of choice is expanded and they can and will *be* more.[4]

3

interplay of faith and economic values

The bourgeoisie, during its rule of scarce one hundred years, has created more massive and more colossal productive forces than have all preceding generations together. Subjection of nature's forces to man, machinery, application of chemistry to industry and agriculture, steam navigation, railways, electric telegraphs, clearing of whole continents for cultivation, canalization of rivers, whole populations conjured out of the ground —what earlier century had even a presentiment that such productive forces slumbered in the lap of social labor?

—Karl Marx and Friedrich Engels
The Communist Manifesto, 1848

Samuel Adams of Boston had a vision for the coming new nation. When the American Revolution had effectively ended the harsh rule of the British, a republic would emerge, on the order of a "Christian Sparta." In a bold new start, the Americans would be a people made strong by discipline and frugality, excelling in the wise management of scarce goods. All this would be nurtured by their faith, a Christianity which cultivated self-denial and rejected sensual and material self-indulgence.

Samuel Adams' vision of a new Sparta came to nought. So did the version of American Christianity he espoused. Why?

Partly, perhaps, because of the enormous productivity that followed the Industrial Revolution and the triumph of the new economics—capitalism. Even the most ardent foes of capitalism, such as Marx and Engels, stood in awe of the accomplishments of the rising commercial class. Such material gains could hardly help but fashion something other than a Christian Sparta in the new land.

Yet all along the way there was a continuous interplay of religious and economic influences in the shaping of American character. At times the interplay is intense and close. Other times a cultural distance separates religious and economic influences. That, too, has shaped our national character. The purpose of this chapter is to trace these varied dynamics.

THE PROTESTANT ETHIC AND YANKEE CAPITALISM

Early in this century Max Weber published an important work, *The Protestant Ethic and the Spirit of Capitalism*. He argued that the Reformation, especially Calvinism, gave rise to a way of life that matched the needs of early commercial and industrial society. That society needed a people who would work hard, lead frugal lives, and save money, postponing the pleasures of leisure and abhoring habits of high consumption. This would permit the accumulation of capital and supply the reliable labor necessary for establishing a broad, solid industrial and commercial base. The ethic needed, then, would make frugality and hard work the cardinal virtues and idleness and material indulgence the cardinal vices. This was "the Protestant Ethic."

The Protestant Ethic had a firm religious base. Its "script" read something like this: "Your arena of service to God is in your day-to-day life. Glorify your Creator and Judge in your workaday world. Faithful performance there is your responsibility before a holy God. Do not indulge in sensual and material delights. Extravagant living is not godly; disciplined self-denial is. Idleness is an abomination. You may indeed accrue wealth as the outcome of hard work and disciplined living. If so, this is a sign of God's favor. Yet, because this world is a harsh and brutal place, you may remain poor in material matters. If so, be assured God will reward your ardent labors with an abundant life on the other side of death."

Worthy of special note is this: In the Protestant Ethic prosperity is a sign of God's favor, as it is in some Old Testament passages. Poverty is not a sign of moral depravity, but idleness in the face of the opportunity to work is.

There is a clear picture of the good life here, the life of giving glory to God in productive labor. There is also a picture of the good person, the responsible steward who is humble, grateful, industrious. These were the moral models in a religious vision that had strong economic consequences in the New World.

But something happened. As industrial society extended itself, changes occurred in the Protestant Ethic, especially in America. A dynamic capitalism requires ever greater capital accumulation, new markets, and higher and higher levels of consumption. As this transpired in the 19th and 20th centuries, one element of the Protestant

Ethic was retained, and other elements were changed. Retained was the enormously productive work ethic. Changed were three components:

1. The frugal simple life-style of deferred pleasures was abandoned, especially in the prosperous decades following World War II.

2. Prosperity became a sign of divine favor and moral accomplishment. Millions of Americans agreed with Episcopal Bishop William Lawrence that "godliness is in league with riches" and that "the gospel of wealth" proclaims two positive principles: "that man, when he is strong, conquers Nature," and that "it is only to the man of morality that wealth comes." [1]

3. Poverty, and not simply idleness, became the clear mark of moral depravity and failure. Henry Ward Beecher, perhaps America's foremost 19th-century preacher, spoke for many:

> Looking comprehensively through city and town and village and country, the general truth will stand, that no man in this land suffers from poverty unless it be more than his fault—unless it be his sin. . . . There is enough and to spare thrice over; and if men have not enough, it is owing to the want of provident care, and foresight, and industry, and frugality, and wise saying. This is the general truth. [2]

With these three changes Americans fashioned an ethic that bordered on divine sanction for the prosperity of the rich and divine condemnation for the poverty of the poor. The Protestant Ethic had in fact been transformed into a Yankee work ethic and a Yankee wealth ethic.

There is irony here. The Protestant Ethic itself unleashed

forces that helped transform it into a work-and-wealth ethic. John Wesley puzzled over how a religious ethic that energized capitalism could avoid undoing itself. He wrote in his *Journals:*

> I fear, whatever riches have increased, the essence of religion has decreased in the same proportion. Therefore I do not see how it is possible, in the nature of things, for any revival of true religion to continue long. For religion must necessarily produce both industry and frugality, and these cannot but produce riches. But as riches increase, so will pride, anger, and love of the world in all its branches. How then is it possible that Methodism, that is, a religion of the heart, though it flourishes now as a green bay tree, should continue in this state? For the Methodists in every place grow diligent and frugal; consequently they increase in goods. Hence, they proportionately increase in pride, in anger, in the desire of the flesh, the desire of the eyes, and the pride of life. So, although the form of religion remains, the spirit is swiftly vanishing away. Is there no way to prevent this—this continual decay of pure religion? We ought not to prevent people from being diligent and frugal; *we must exhort all Christians to gain all they can, and to save all they can; that is, in effect, to grow rich.*[3]

Wesley goes on to his famed advice that those who gain and save all they can should give away all they can. But this was utterly inadequate for stemming indulgence in the riches believed to be the fruit of "true religion."

"True religion," was, of course, not all religion. In the U.S. it was the Protestantism found in Calvinist New England, Quaker Pennsylvania, Methodist and Baptist frontier regions, and Midwest-immigrant Lutheranism. It was, in Max Weber's words:

> the religious valuation of restless, continuous, systematic work in a worldly setting, as the highest means to asceticism, and at the same time the surest and most evident proof of . . . genuine faith.[4]

When this was combined with the economic needs of youthful capitalism in a setting of great material resources, the results were about as inevitable as any in history. Again in Weber's words:

> When the limitation on consumption is combined with this release of acquisitive activity, the inevitable practical result is obvious: accumulation of capital through ascetic compulsion to save. The restraints which were imposed upon the consumption to wealth naturally served to increase it by making possible the productive investment of capital.[5]

In a word, the Protestant Ethic manifested itself in economic life as a driving propensity to accumulation. What began in asceticism (discipline, self-denial, frugality) ended up in hedonism *as soon as the religious restraint on consumption loosened.* And, as Wesley perceived, this religious restraint was loosened by the very riches it generated. What began in simplicity ended in luxury. The Protestant Ethic helped generate a driving Yankee riches ethic.

Of course, there were other influences shaping American character and economic life. One was the individualism that seemed to thrive on frontier soil. It emphasized personal responsibility and self-reliance. This individualism was given a particular form as capitalism took root. In the classic text of capitalism's morality, *The Wealth of Nations*, published in 1776, Adam Smith formulated the contention that caught on. The individual acting in his own interest, Smith asserted, would do that which would also be in the best interest of all. "The Invisible Hand" would orchestrate life in such a way that individual self-interest in economic life would also serve the common good.

This ethic of capitalist individualism took root in America to a depth almost unparalleled elsewhere. It soon became more than just an economic ethic. It became a spirit pervading much of the social life. In a setting of increasing abundance, it evolved into an ethic of a virtually unrestrained pursuit of individual happiness. Personal happiness became the purpose of economic endeavor, replacing the Protestant Ethic's goal of giving glory to God in productive labor. In the recent setting of prosperity, this happiness has been measured by leisure-time pleasure, marked by material accumulation, and pursued by the high consumption of resources of all kinds. The work ethic has largely given way to a consumption ethic.

PIETISM AND SECULARIZATION

Still other streams of influence are discernible in American religious and economic life. Lutheranism, especially that of Scandinavian and German immigrants, was strongly influenced by the movement known as pietism. It developed in Europe as a response to what was considered an unfeeling and overly-intellectual understanding of faith as "right belief" or "correct doctrine."

Pietism was essentially a matter of having one's "heart strangely warmed" (John Wesley's phrase, describing his own experience in the Methodist revival movement that arose somewhat later). Faith was a matter of personal experience and feeling. What mattered most was one's living relationship with a personal God. So self and God, personal sin, the experience of grace and forgiveness, and individual testimony were the hallmarks of true religion. True religion had to do with the inner lives of people and not with institutions or with society's major preoccupations, such as politics and economics. For pietism, religious life and political/economic life were two different arenas.

Secularization, a social process that has occurred in all industrial nations, has been another stream of influence. In the course of industrialization, certain arenas of life have come to have their own "rules of the game," their own dynamics and institutional arrangements. Politics is politics; economics is economics; family life is family life; and religion is religion, a separate sphere only tangentially related to the others. Religion does not mix in a major way with economic life—and is not supposed to.

Pietism and secularization reinforced one another. Pietism made of religion a private and personal matter. This encouraged secularization's removal of religion from the rough-and-tumble of economic and political life—a place religion did hold in Samuel Adam's vision, in Adam Smith's theorizing, and in colonial Calvinism. So from both directions religious choices became more and more matters of personal preference that had less and less to do with economic matters.

SPIRITUALIZING THE MATERIAL

Another stream that runs deep in American religious life has its own outcome for economics. The origins are in the Western Christian heritage. In Christianity (much more than in Judaism) the biblical references to food and health, poverty and riches, goods and the good have been "spiritualized"; that is, concrete material realities have been rendered as nonmaterial ones. The hungry become those hungry for God's Word, or the poor become the poor in spirit. The naked become those exposed in their sin before God; the imprisoned, those in bondage to sin; the ill are sick in soul; the blind are the spiritually undiscerning. Salvation is regarded as a matter of the soul, which is divorced from the body. Then religion becomes a matter of spiritual values, on a different plane from material matters —like economic life.

This process of spiritualizing, though understandable, is extraordinary, given Jewish and Christian origins. For the Bible knows no such division of material from spiritual, or body from soul, but only what might be called "embodied spirit" and "animated body." Salvation, in Scripture, has many meanings. Liberation from economic and political oppression is a major one, as is "wholeness" or "full health." But all the meanings include material dimensions inseparable from dimensions that transcend the material.

Langdon Gilkey reports an incident that reflects not only this tendency to spiritualize, but many of the other tendencies in American religious and economic life that we have described. Gilkey had been asked to address a church group about the moral dilemmas he and others faced when interned by the Japanese during World War II.

> [We] met in a mammoth suburban residence outside Chicago, the expansive driveway lined with black Cadillacs and

Lincolns. This group contained some forty middle-aged women, elegantly dressed and adorned.

As I spoke to these smiling and gracious ladies in the living room, out of the corner of my eye I could see two or three maids putting sandwiches, cookies, and towering chocolate cakes on the dining room table. I suppose I stressed the problems of hunger and the need for sharing even more than usual as my eye traveled from minks to gentle, round faces, to chauffeurs pacing outside, and then back to the cakes again. When I had finished, the president, whose face had worn a slight frown during the latter course of my talk, called for questions. When none were proffered, she rose and addressed the following remarks to me.

"I think our visitor, for all his good intentions, does not understand our point of view on these matters. You see, we don't believe at all in the value of material things. It is the spiritual values of life that we feel are significant. We believe that what America has to offer the world is her spiritual superiority, not any advantage she may have in the realm of mere material goods. Thus we would like to encourage the export to Europe and the rest of the world of our great spiritual ideals, our religious faith, our sense of morality and of the value of the inner life. So we send moral and religious writings abroad, and do not approve of concentrating on the things that are not so important to the welfare of the soul. . . . If there are, then, no more questions, let us adjourn the meeting. I can see our hostess has provided us with tantalizing refreshments." [6]

STUDY PROJECT

This chapter has described some of the ways that American religious and economic developments have interacted, either directly or at some distance from one another. In light of this chapter and your own experience and knowledge, what would you identify as the religious, ethical, and economic values underlying the following phrases or sentiments?

1. Standard of living.
2. Well-off.
3. "I just can't buy that idea."
4. "God helps those who help themselves."
5. "It's our money so we can do with it as we please."
6. "We repudiate the charge that we have exploited or plundered other countries, or that our own prosperity has ever rested upon any such relation. We are prosperous because we are—or were—an energetic and productive people who have lived under a system that has encouraged the development of our productive capacities and energies" (Daniel Patrick Moynihan, in a speech to the AFL-CIO when he was U.S. Ambassador to the United Nations).
7. "I came that they may have life, and have it abundantly" (John 10:10).
8. "We've been richly blessed and we're thankful for our blessings. But if you look around you'll find a lot of

genuine spiritual poverty and hunger among the prosperous people in this neighborhood. I think the job of the
churches is to minister to the deep unhappiness that's
here."

9. "In the end you get what you deserve, you reap
what you sow, you get out of something what you put
into it. As far as I can see, it's the same with countries,
too."

10. "See that beautiful shell over there? Wonder what
it's worth."

4

interplay of economic values and culture

Religion brought forth prosperity; and then the daughter destroyed the mother.
—Cotton Mather
Magnalia Christi Americana, 1702

All but one of [the seven deadly] sins, sloth, was transformed into a positive virtue. Greed, avarice, envy, gluttony, luxury, and pride were the driving forces of the new economy. Goals and ends capable of working an inner transformation were obsolete; mechanical expansion itself had become the supreme goal.
—Lewis Mumford
The Transformations of Man, 1956

The time from Mather's writing (the 17th and 18th centuries) through Mumford's (the 20th century) saw the rise of "modern culture." Many refer to it simply as the age of "Economic Man" [1] or "the making of economic society." It is a culture dominated by a robust economic life.

Carl Sandburg's poem, "Chicago," catches much of the

ethos: the pounding urban drive, the continuous, pulsating transformation of both nature and society, the extension of energy-intensive technology to all sectors, including agriculture, and the strong male giantism of economic man's culture. "Chicago" begins:

> Hog Butcher for the World,
> Tool Maker, Stacker of Wheat,
> Player with Railroads and the Nation's Freight Handler
> Stormy, husky, brawling,
> City of the Big Shoulders:

Then, after admitting the seamy side of "progress"— violence, poverty—the poet offers a defense:

> Come and show me another city with lifted head singing so proud to be alive and coarse and strong and cunning.
> Flinging magnetic curses amid the toil of piling job on job, here is a tall bold slugger set vivid against the little soft cities;
> Fierce as a dog with tongue lapping for action, cunning as a savage pitted against the wilderness,
> Bareheaded,
> Shoveling,
> Wrecking,
> Planning,
> Building, breaking, rebuilding.[2]

This kind of throbbing economic messianism has been characteristic of both industrial capitalism and industrial socialism, a fact we shall detail in the next chapter. Here the attention is centered on American capitalism and its impact on this culture and its morality. What is the connection between "modern culture" and this society's economic life?

The Protestant Ethic provided a religious ethos and a moral code that aided and abetted the rise of early capitalism. But the Protestant Ethic emerged in a society that *preceded* the modern industrial order.

Something of great significance rests in this fact. The societal foundations of capitalism were laid in a society not of capitalism's own making and perhaps even at odds with it. It may well be that a capitalist order, once firmly established, nurtures a concept of "the good life" quite different from that of the foundations on which it was built. Perhaps capitalism undercuts its own cultural and moral footings.

Ronald Preston notes that capitalism began with heavy reliance on certain virtues: commitments to honesty and trust, a respect for law, and a sense of obligation to prevent fraud, theft, and breach of contract.[3] The source of these was not in the capitalist organization of economic life, but in other sources that preceded it: the traditional social ties of face-to-face relationships, pervasive religious teaching, and a strong sense of civic duty.[4]

The question is whether capitalism has continued to foster these or to erode them, offering some other profile of the good life. Lewis Mumford clearly believes that the virtues on which American capitalism rested for its establishment were not the ones it continued to sanction. Nor were the vices long deplored. As he pointed out, American capitalism glorified six of the seven deadly sins, excluding only sloth.

FREEDOM AND THE PORTABLE SELF

Daniel Bell's definition of "modern culture" merits careful reading:

> "Modern culture" is defined by [the] extraordinary freedom to ransack the world storehouse and to engorge any and every style it comes upon. Such freedom comes from the fact that the axial principle of modern culture is the expression and remaking of the "self" in order to achieve self-realization and self-fulfillment. And in its search, there is a denial of any limits or boundaries to experience. It is a reaching out for all experience; nothing is forbidden, all is to be explored.[5]

The "axial principle of modern culture" has thrived on a notion of freedom in which freedom is essentially freedom *from* limits and constraints and *for* self-achieved self-fulfillment. The roots are deep in the American psyche. They have lived on even when the particular moral values and the reigning religious ethos have changed markedly. Benjamin Franklin's *Autobiography*, widely read in Colonial America, lists 13 prize virtues: temperance, order, resolution, frugality, industry, sincerity, silence, justice, moderation, cleanliness, tranquility, chastity, and humility. Franklin testified that he gave a week's attention to each, jotting daily progress in his journal. Since there were 13 virtues, he completed his course in character-building four times a year.

The major point is not the character-building, or even the list of virtues, although they accord well with the needs of early capitalism. The line that runs steadily from Benjamin Franklin to a thousand self-help groups today is the tradition of *self-managed self-improvement* or self-effected self-fulfillment.

The capitalist order may not of itself call for this, but in the United States that order has been surrounded and supported by a philosophy of political and economic individualism that does. C. B. Macpherson's summary of this outlook, here condensed further, is almost an American creed:

> 1. What makes people human is freedom from dependence on the wills of others.
>
> 2. Freedom from dependence on others means freedom from any relations with others except those relations which individuals enter voluntarily with a view to their own interests.
>
> 3. Individuals are essentially the proprietors of their own person and capacities, for which they owe nothing to society.
>
> 4. Human society consists of a series of market relations.
>
> 5. Since freedom from the wills of others is what makes one human, each individual's freedom can rightly be limited only by such obligations and rules as are necessary to secure the same freedom for others.
>
> 6. Political society is a human contrivance for the protection of individuals' property in their person and goods, and [therefore] for the maintenance of orderly relations of exchange between individuals regarded as proprietors themselves.[6]

In short, we are on our own, and society is essentially a series of market relations. Everything is converted into a commodity for the market, not only goods, but labor and services as well. They are for purchase, and the individual pursues self-realization and self-fulfillment by "shopping around."

Individualism comes in many modes. This one holds a particular view of the self: the imperial self. The world is outside oneself and is seen as an object over against, or apart from, the self. The world is the "stuff" to be transformed by humans in the service of individual self-pursuits. It is a "storehouse" for the individual seeking self-realization, the place that houses infinite materials for a *making* and *doing* self. The world is malleable, to be "thrown" as a potter "throws" clay, in accord with human design. The self is a mastering and controlling, rather than receiving, self—"wrecking, planning, building, breaking, rebuilding."

With such a perspective, reinforced by the incentives of the capitalist system, it is not happenstance that the dominant figures in 19th century America were the entrepreneur, the engineer and industrialist, and the frontier settler.

Some point to the 1960s and '70s as a turn away from "Economic Man" and the imperial self, and a turn toward the "inner transformation" Mumford missed in the preoccupation of the '50s with "mechanical expansion." "Psychological Man" has succeeded "Economic Man."

Yet this is a shift, rather than a displacement, of the cultural spirit; it is still imperial individualism in quest of self-managed self-fulfillment working on a world seen as malleable and unlimited. Only now the world is "within" as well as "without," "inner" as well as "outer." Note carefully the language used to advertise a service at an American university:

> Interpersonal Skill-Building Groups: In these 10-session skill-focused groups, students will be taught to monitor and master

> anxiety, using . . . improved social skills
> by learning to be appropriately assertive.[7]

The same offer speaks of "designing experiences" and acquiring skills "to establish trust."[8] This language of building in a world where experiences can be *designed* and trust *established,* assertiveness *learned* and anxiety *monitored* and *mastered*—all this is the tradition, albeit in varied form, that runs from Franklin's *Autobiography* all the way to the many "workshops" of the 1970s.

The imperial sense of self and the marketplace individualism are not the only ways in which American economic life expresses itself. The economic order is restless, and that, too, has its strong influence on the sense of self. In part because of shifting job locations and markets, Americans are a people on the move.

This makes for what psychologist Robert Weigl calls "the portable self." People on the go, he finds, often have a certain confidence: "I can find a niche for myself wherever I am." But they also lack "deep attachments to the place and people where they live" and show "tenuous communication" and "tremendous alienation and distrust of their environment." They may join in temporary association for some common causes—a school tax issue, for example. But the bonds are not lasting, and close friendships do not flower. "They are very poor in asking help from their neighbors."[9]

What worries Weigl most is the absence of "long-term, slowly evolved, interfamiliar ties" that could provide "exchanges of concern, comfort, information and material aid." Too many fundamental needs "for intimacy, self-disclosure, self-affirmation and letting your hair down all have to be met in that half-acre lot, in that 2,700-square-foot bilevel that looked so gratifying when first shown by the realtor."

Some people negotiate the transiency rather well, but some do not, and the incidence of alcoholism, divorce, child neglect, depression, and a restless unhappiness runs high. Weigl concludes: "We are not infinitely plastic and movable, and to a very considerable extent our ongoing sense of ourselves is our lasting bonds to our human and physical environment."

The poet T. S. Eliot has a response to "Chicago," this unceasing activity of the imperial self on the go, this fast-paced making and remaking of the world.

> The endless cycle of ideas and action,
> Endless invention, endless experiment,
> Brings knowledge of motion, but not of
>   stillness;
> Knowledge of speech, but not of silence;
> Knowledge of words, and ignorance of
>   the Word.[10]

LIMITS AND EXPERIENCE

The cultural impact of American capitalism over 150 years and more cannot be understood apart from a recognition of its almost unique setting: peoples imbued with the drive of "Chicago" settled a vast, sparsely populated continent of enormous wealth. Such a setting bequeathed us a deeply ingrained sense of the unlimited.

The change of meaning for the word "frontier" is illustrative of this mindset. For most societies, and certainly preindustrial ones, "frontier" meant a formidable limit, a stopping place, a forbidding region uninhabitable and uninviting. It signaled the halting edge of conquest and marked the boundary for making do with what one had. But for aggressive industrialism in general and for Americans in particular, "frontier" has come to mean virtually the opposite: not the stopping place but the next starting place, a challenge to expansion and an invitation to conquest. So we set out to "conquer space" or wage a "war on poverty." Above all, it has meant, not "making do," but the acquisition of more—more land, more resources, more wealth, more room, for opportunities.[12]

American capitalism lives on this expansive spirit and in turn nourishes it. The economic order has, in fact, institutionalized it. In any event, it is a general cultural trait; we crave an unbounded culture and have a difficult time saying *yes* to any limits. *All* is to be explored.

Thus a common "catechism" for an American child, at least for a white male, might go something like this:

> Gather to yourself all you can—experience, knowledge, goods, skills. Make your own world, as you see fit, and enjoy. Grow for all your worth, in every way. Never close off any options. Nothing is forbidden, all is to be explored.

Not likely to be heard is a "catechism" common to many long-standing religious traditions:

> You will find yourself with needs that cannot be satisfied and wants that cannot be fulfilled. There are circumstances beyond your control and fears not easily appeased. So learn courage, endurance, and patience. Recognize powers beyond your own, and accept the world with joy.

Despite the current economic tightening, this "engorg [ing] [of] any and every style" without any sense of moderation and restraint is so much a part of us that one finds it by leafing through any mass-circulation magazine.

Here is one such ad, and with it we can bring this chapter to a close, since it illustrates most of our themes:

In the ad a young woman of sexy expression and dress says:

> Everything in moderation is about the dullest philosophy I ever heard! Without any *question* I work "too hard"—at least nine hours a day, sometimes ten. I definitely care too much for Lionel (Isn't that a crazy name?!) my husband, but Lionel is my reward at the end of the day for "working too hard." I also cook too passionately and play tennis to win, and on my last birthday I ate *forty* bluepoint oysters. My favorite magazine says don't worry about "too much" as long as the "too much" makes you feel utterly fulfilled, utterly utilized, and usually, utterly happy. I love that magazine. I guess you could say I'm That *Cosmopolitan* Girl.[13]

STUDY PROJECT

This chapter, like the others, addresses the theme of economic doubt. But here it is of a somewhat different kind. The concern is the connection between American capitalism and the notion of "the good life" it fosters. What is the cultural impact of our economic order and the habits of character and conduct it encourages? Are they the ones pointed to in this chapter, or are there others? If they include those of this chapter, how does that tally with your picture of "the good life"?

Readers may wish to continue the discussion of American capitalism's impact on culture. Many materials might be chosen, but "Chicago" by Carl Sandburg is a good place to begin. How are the economic order and ethos intertwined with the cultural spirit expressed in the poem?

CHICAGO

Hog Butcher for the World,
Tool Maker, Stacker of Wheat,
Player with Railroads and the Nation's Freight
    Handler;
Stormy, husky, brawling,
City of the Big Shoulders:

They tell me you are wicked and I believe them, for I have seen your painted women under the gas lamps luring the farm boys.

And they tell me you are crooked and I answer: Yes, it is true I have seen the gunman kill and go free to kill again.

And they tell me you are brutal and my reply is: On the faces of women and children I have seen the marks of wanton hunger.

And having answered so I turn once more to those who sneer at this my city, and I give them back the sneer and say to them:

Come and show me another city with lifted head singing so proud to be alive and coarse and strong and cunning.

Flinging magnetic curses amid the toil of piling job on job, here is a tall bold slugger set vivid against the little soft cities;

Fierce as a dog with tongue lapping for action, cunning as a savage pitted against the wilderness,
    Bareheaded,
    Shoveling,
    Wrecking,

Planning,
Building, breaking, rebuilding,
Under the smoke, dust all over his mouth, laughing with white teeth,
Under the terrible burden of destiny laughing as a young man laughs,
Laughing even as an ignorant fighter laughs who has never lost a battle,
Bragging and laughing that under his wrist is the pulse, and under his ribs the heart of the people,
Laughing!
Laughing the stormy, husky, brawling laughter of Youth, half-naked, sweating, proud to be Hog Butcher, Tool Maker, Stacker of Wheat, Player with Railroads and Freight Handler to the Nation.

5

capitalisms and socialisms

The political problem of mankind is to combine three things: economic efficiency, social justice, and individual liberty.
　　　　　　　—John Maynard Keynes
　　　　　　　Liberalism and Labour, 1926

Economic life after World War II is markedly different from the preceding decades. Before, there were two dominant models in the industrialized world. The capitalist model, exemplified by Great Britain and the United States, was one. The socialist model, exemplified by the Soviet Union, was the other.

The postwar decades brought important adaptations, so many that the Table of Contents of any book on economic systems today includes an array of choices. For example: "The Case for Marxism," "The Case for Laissez-Faire Capitalism," "The Case for Social Market Capitalism," "The Case for Democratic Socialism," "The Case for Economic Conservationism." [1]

One reason for the proliferation of economic systems rests in the teachings of experience. The capitalist countries suffered the trauma of the Depression of the 1930s and learned from it. Part of what was learned was successful planned economic intervention undertaken or guided by government. So when capitalist nations emerged from the '40s, they showed the marks of a different capitalism, one with managed fiscal policy and many "welfare state" services.

The earlier socialism learned from history, too, but a very different lesson: that an economy could be strangled by tight, centralized planning and unwieldy bureaucracies. Many socialist nations undertook experiments with limited decentralization and the introduction of some economic incentives usually associated with capitalist systems.

Another reason for the greater variety of economic systems was the impact of different peoples and cultures on the systems they adopted. When Japan and Germany underwent their postwar reconstruction, they fashioned capitalisms quite different from that of the U.S. Yet it was hardly socialism; it was simply Japanese and German capitalism. And when the Chinese, the Yugoslavs, and the Cubans adopted Marxism-Leninism, they did so in ways different from that of the U.S.S.R. and from each other as well. Now there are at least a dozen socialist or communist economies, just as there are a dozen capitalist economies.

All this makes comparison of capitalism and socialism difficult. Who exemplifies "true" capitalism? Is it Brazil, Switzerland, Great Britain, Japan, Kenya, the U.S., South Korea, South Africa, or the Federal Republic of Germany? And who exemplifies "true" socialism? The Soviet Union, the People's Republic of China, Cuba, Yugoslavia, Mozambique, Hungary, or the German Democratic Republic? And are the Swedes and the Dutch and the Danes "democratic socialists" or "welfare capitalists"? Or is there a meaningful difference between these two terms?

There is a third reason for the large number of economic models, one hinted at in our list of countries. Prior to World War II, few emerging nations had taken on the task of fashioning their own economic orders. Indeed, their national economies were so closely tied to those of the colonial powers that they were not even a separate subject. Today, many developing nations are trying to fashion economic patterns quite different from those which have dominated this century.

Soviet economists have a term for this effort. They call it "non-capitalist development." It is not capitalist, but it is also not Marxist; it fits neither of the classic models. The prominent marks are these: extensive nationalization of industry and finance, various social welfare measures, government regulation of small and medium capitalists, heightened attention to rural development, and non-alignment politics that usually includes an appeal for aid and trade with nations of various persuasions—socialist, capitalist, or otherwise.[2] The Republic of Tanzania is an example of this profile.

It may be, as some say, that such countries will have to choose to become either more markedly capitalist or more genuinely socialist. What is clear, however, is that many of the smaller, poorer nations no longer regard the economic models of richer, industrialized nations as appropriate and desirable for them. So they have undertaken their own experiments, which adds to the confusing array of economic orders present today.

That array should not leave us confused, however. Nor should it obscure the fact that there are identifiable characteristics of capitalism and socialism. There are clear and meaningful differences.

CAPITALISM

Present-day capitalism has three basic characteristics. Two are distinctly different from those of socialism, and one is held jointly.

1. The means of production are owned by private citizens, whether as sole owners of a business or farm, or as stockholders in corporations of varying size, from small to huge.

2. The economy is dominated by what are called "market transactions." That means that every breadwinner in a capitalist order acquires a livelihood by selling something of market value. Resources, goods, services, labor, skills, and even information and ideas are all offered for purchase in the market. Thus, all production in a modern capitalist order revolves around commercial buying and selling. People offer something of money-value, including themselves, to the market.

3. Industrialization is the third strong mark of modern capitalism.

To speak of capitalism today means, then, to speak of an industrialized order in which the means of production are privately owned and in which a market system dominates.

The original capitalism of Adam Smith had a clear moral premise: that individual self-interest is the prime motivator of human action and that the most efficient economy is one in which this self-interest is given free play. In other words, human nature is such that, as the Darwinians put it, "free competition had built Man," and free competition in the marketplace would also produce the most economizing choices and secure the greatest material achievement.

In pure form, this laissez-faire, free-enterprise capitalism has never existed on a large scale. From early on, governments have intervened. The reasons are multiple, but perhaps the most important has been the unplanned consequences of capitalism. George Dalton notes:

> No one decided that there should be children working 14 hours a day in factories, adulterated food, dysentery and cholera from bad city water, noxious factory smoke, sporadic unemployment, or crime in cities. They were the unintended results of using the new machinery to produce goods in the cheapest way for national and international markets, or the result of the new urban working and living conditions created by factories, large urban populations, and dependence for livelihood on competitive markets.[3]

Dalton also notes that wherever the industrialist-capitalist society of "massive factories, markets and cities" has spread, the same kinds of governmental interventions and social services have followed: workers' compensation, health care provisions, safety regulations, social security, and public services of various kinds.

The 1930s and '40s transformed whatever was left of the near laissez-faire capitalism of the 19th century. Government moved from a sometime intervener and aide to capitalism, to guide and manager of much of the capitalist order. A host of measures were—and are—used, aimed chiefly at sustaining economic growth and promoting employment. The crucial fact is, as conservative economist Milton Friedman put it, "We are all Keynesians now." Government policy, influenced by British economist Lord Keynes, plays a large role in the manipulation of a capitalist economy in order to combat harsh depression and curb recession and inflation.

SOCIALISM

Modern socialism arose from within the industrialized order that capitalism built. It is Western in origin and came into being when capitalist orders were seeking to avoid or to repair the harsh consequences of industrialization and urbanization. It was not coincidental that Karl Marx did much of his work in the homeland of the Industrial Revolution, 19th-century Britain. And it was not an accident that socialist parties, Marxist and otherwise, proliferated throughout industrial Europe in that same century.

Because socialism arose as a reformist or revolutionary response to the evils of capitalism, it has been as much a social critique as an alternative economic scheme. In fact, Marx sought an alternative *because* he judged capitalism to be humanly degrading and riddled with social injustice. The many smaller movements of "Christian socialism" or "religious socialism" that have come and gone over the last two centuries have been impelled by the same criticism of capitalism.

Yet socialism has not gathered its strongest following in advanced capitalist settings. Most socialist orders have in fact come about in countries with only "infant" capitalism (such as the U.S.S.R.) or in noncapitalist and rural societies (such as China). Typically, a dramatic class structure has been present, often one of wealthy landowners and business families over against a desperately poor peasantry.

Socialist economic schemes vary widely from one to another. There have been many kinds: Marxist, German and Scandinavian democratic, English democratic, and guild socialism, to name a few. Even within the dominant type, Marxist socialism, there has been considerable diversity, often generating intense conflict between Marxists. Yet modern socialism, any kind, has two marks that set it apart from capitalism:

1. The collective ownership of the means of production (in contrast to private ownership), directed by government.

2. The dominance of centralized governmental planning in the economy (in contrast to the dominance of market mechanisms).

Most major socialist powers share with capitalism the third major characteristic—the decisive place of industrialization.

Historians note that capitalist orders have adopted many socialist planks. Perhaps we could say that "we are all socialists now." The *Communist Manifesto's* call for a graduated income tax and publicly-financed education for all children is in no danger of repeal today as "communist-inspired." Similarly, social security and old-age pensions, subsidized or socialized medicine, paid vacations and regulated working hours, child-labor laws and minimum wage standards, are all common fare for both socialist and capitalist societies. It is also true that socialist nations have adopted typically capitalist planks such as private production for a free market in some food commodities.

THE CONVERGENCE

These common policies have led some to speak of a *convergence* of modern capitalism and socialism. The case is bolstered by adding that capitalism has given an expanding place to government regulation of the economy while socialism has learned the virtue of introducing some market mechanisms into its economies.

Yet these converging tendencies should not obscure important differences, which go to the heart of the two basic schemes. Welfare capitalism does indeed use extensive central-government power in the economy. But it is still capitalism because production is privately owned, and the market determines the allocation of resources and incomes in a major way. Democratic socialism, which looks so similar to welfare capitalism, is still socialism because production is nationalized, and the economy centrally planned in a way that casts market mechanisms into a secondary role.

There is convergence, but it is of a different sort and has only recently received due notice. It is this, underscored by George Dalton:

> Highly developed industrial countries share basic features regardless of whether they are capitalist or communist. . . . Agricultural employment, the share of agricultural output in GNP and rural residence all decline; urbanization, factory employment and the provision of services grow; birth rates and death rates decline; literacy becomes universal and the proportion of the population receiving education beyond elementary school increases; modern technology and applied science come to be employed in all producing sectors; regional differences in income and in social capital within each country diminish; growth in GNP per capita is built in.[5]

Also built in, Dalton goes on, is a vast array of common afflictions and negative conditions. Both industrial socialist and capitalist orders face severe deterioration of their physical environment. Air, land, and water pollution plague East as well as West. Both face the common constraints of diminishing resources. They share a growing energy crisis. Both have been strongly growth-oriented economies, both have held an almost unquestioned faith in science and technology, and both will have to confront the limits-to-growth factors they have generally ignored.

There are also similar social and psychological disorders. Alienation and a scarcity of satisfactions mark the lives of millions in both systems, neither bringing about its promised fulfillment of the human spirit. Divorce, alcoholism, suicide, and crime seem to have grown with urban living, increased incomes, and higher consumption in both kinds of society.

Both have shared a common illusion. They assumed that an economy of abundance would eliminate the causes for destructive rivalry that afflict an economy of scarcity. Neither had an understanding "for the perennial conflicts of power and pride which may arise on every level of 'abundance' since human desires grow with the means of their gratification." [6]

The question in the early '80s is whether present "conflicts of power and pride" *between* major capitalist and socialist powers are bringing about another common development *within* their economies. Many signs point to a transition in both camps from a welfare state to a national security state. The shift is away from an economy of expanding social services and toward a defense economy. A mood of expansiveness is giving way to a mood of get, hold, and keep. An international economic life increasingly troubled over coming lean years seems to go hand-in-hand with an aggressive protectionist spirit within national economies, whether capitalist or socialist.

A brief summary, then, is this: Both capitalism and socialism have been, and are, undergoing much change, taking on different forms in different places. As industrialized societies, they show some common marks, as well as some continuing differences. They also share some common afflictions that underscore what we said at the outset of this study: ours is a time of economic doubt and anxiety, a time when confidence about the organization of economic life has waned.

STUDY PROJECT

This chapter provides no explicit evaluation of current capitalisms and socialisms in light of Christian faith. Readers may wish to undertake one. J. Philip Wogaman's book, *The Great Economic Debate: An Ethical Analysis,* includes a section that serves as a place to begin (pp. 51-53). He lists several criteria that can be used to measure any economic system. Readers may wish to add others.

Wogaman poses five questions to various economic ideologies. We have been speaking of economic systems, but his questions serve our inquiry as well, since the ideologies include the philosophy and the claims put forward by proponents of various capitalisms and socialisms. Here are Wogaman's questions:

1. Does the economic ideology take material well-being itself seriously as a basis for human fulfillment? (Wogaman contends that Christian faith, with its doctrine of creation, does take material well-being seriously.)

2. Is the economic ideology committed to the basic unity of the human family and does its view of economic life measure economic success in terms of the economic undergirding of mutual love in the life of community?

3. Does it include belief in the value of each individual human being, and is it committed to individual freedom and opportunity for individual creative development and expression?

4. Does it consider human beings to be equal in a sense that is more basic than any inequalities, and does this

guide the formulation of economic objectives and policies?

5. Does it take the universality of human sinfulness seriously, and does it make realistic provision for the effects of self-centeredness in its proposed policies? [7]

In Wogaman's view, the more fully a *yes* answer can be given, the more an ideology satisfies the expectations of Christian ethics. In evaluating, readers should choose economic systems they know firsthand. Thus, for most, American capitalism should be one system selected. Every effort should also be made to evaluate a contrasting philosophy. If necessary, recruit resource persons (perhaps faculty or students from overseas at a nearby university or college) or undertake research assignments that will provide knowledge of another economic order.

As an alternative or supplement to the Wogaman list, readers could use the three elements from the Keynes' quotation at the opening of this chapter. Critical judgment of economic systems can be made on the basis of economic efficiency, social justice, and individual liberty.

6

rich
and poor

We are often told that riches are not synonymous with happiness; that life is more than economics. I do not disagree; nor do I challenge the statement that the gross national product of a country fails to indicate the quality of life there. But it is the well-off who can make such statements. To the starving, good and assured food is the quality of life. For a woman who now has to walk miles for water, a village tap might mean life itself.

We are poor; and we stay poor because we are poor—and because the rich are rich. We talk of the Industrialized, the Third, and the Fourth Worlds. But really there is One World. We in the poorest countries are very conscious of the world's unity because we are shaken every day by events which take place, and decisions which are made, thousands of miles from our borders. But ultimately no one is ex-

empted from the effects of poverty and
economic inequalities in the world.
—Julius K. Nyerere
"The Third World and the
International Economic Structure"

For American Christians the basic unit of Christian
thinking about human reality is not "the national interest." It is the *oikoumene,* "the whole inhabited earth in
God," the One World.

Oikoumene is a Greek word, from *oikos* or *house.* *Economics, ecumenical,* and *ecology* are all words that share
this same root. The One World is the house. *Economics*
means providing for the household's needs and managing
it well. *Ecumenical* means seeing the inhabitants as a
single family and fostering the family's unity. *Ecology* refers to the knowledge of that interdependence on which
the life of the house depends. If we add a word from another origin, *stewardship,* the meaning is that of the good
householder whom Jesus describes as one "who brings
out of his treasure what is new and what is old" (Matt.
13:52).

THE WIDENING GAP

If we scan "the whole inhabited earth" today, we see
some brutal realities. Three-fourths of the world's populace are poor. About one-fourth live in absolute poverty.
Approximately 700 million are seriously malnourished,
and millions, mostly children, will die this year from
malnutrition or related causes.[1]

Such statistics numb us. We cannot take in the whole
world at once. Let us for a moment focus just on that part
of the house's population that is Christian. Walter Buehl-

mann has documented some "continental shifts" that are taking place over the course of this century.[2]

	1900	1965	2000 (projected)
Millions of Christians in northern developed countries (e.g., Europe, North America)	392	637	796
Millions of Christians in southern developing countries (Asia, Africa, South America)	67	370	1118

In percentages the distribution looks like this:

	1900	1965	2000
"First" and "Second" Church (northern hemisphere countries of industrial capitalism and industrial socialism)	85%	63%	42%
"Third" Church (in the new nations, chiefly of the southern hemisphere)	15%	37%	58%

The picture is clear: there is a steady and massive increase in the number of Christians who live in the southern developing countries. Yet this is only half the picture. The rest is in the income statistics, where the figures show the stark contrast between wealth and poverty.

Average per capita annual income in dollars, in low-income continents:[3]

	1960	1976
Asia (excl. Japan)	90	290
Africa	105	420
South America	319	1230

Compare this with a poorer country of "the north" (Italy) and two of its richer colleagues. Average per capita annual income in dollars:[4]

	1960	1976
Italy	928	3220
West Germany	1578	7510
United States	3200	7880

Here is the north/south gap. Even a poorer region of the richer hemisphere (Italy) shows almost triple the average income of the poorer hemisphere's richest continent (South America). The contrast in the year 2000 will be even starker. The northern industrialized nations, it is estimated, will then have 1500 million people with average annual incomes of $10,000, while the 4500 million people of the southern nations will have an average annual income of $500, a ratio of about 20:1.[5]

It means the already large gap continues to widen. World Bank President Robert McNamara reports that the developing world's per capita income, adjusted for inflation, increased only $3 for the decade 1970-79, while that of the developed world increased $900.

This is no gap; it is an abyss. If we assume the economic state of Christians reflects that of the populace as a whole, then the picture looks like this: Nearly a majority of the world's Christians are poor, and many of them live in absolute poverty. At the same time, among the world's richest peoples, Christianity is the dominant faith. Within their own ranks, then, Christians mirror the global realities: the poor are the majority, the rich are the overprivileged few.

REASONS FOR THE GAP

Both rich and poor have been aware of the plague of poverty, of course. There have been major movements to understand and change the mechanisms that seem to generate wealth in one hemisphere and poverty in the other.

Yet any "solution" depends heavily upon what "the problem" really is. And here disagreement prevails. Several explanations exist.

Some say the root is an economic *neo-colonialism* that continued after the poor countries gained their political independence. The less-developed countries remain the source of cheap raw materials and cheap labor that are exploited to feed the high-consumption habits of the industrial nations. Large transnational corporations are the vehicles for moving wealth from the poor to the rich, as well as among the rich themselves. Often there are politically and economically powerful people within the poor nations who benefit from these arrangements. But their existence is tied closely to the economics and life-styles of wealthy foreign nations, and so they, too, are part of the neo-colonialist structure.

Another view regards the problem as essentially one of unequal opportunities, chiefly in trade. The poor countries, while dependent on trade, lack any leverage in determining the price they receive for their exports or the price they pay for needed imports. (The oil-exporting countries are an exception, and they are no longer poor, in GNP per capita.) One example will illustrate a common experience. Between 1970 and 1974 the average prices of East Africa's five major export commodities went up 34%. During the same period the cost of their industrial imports went up 91%. The point is not only the worsening exchange. It is that the rich countries, and not East African nations, had the power to determine the prices of the poor nations' exports and their imports.

A third view claims that the problem is the lack of capital and slow growth in the developing countries. Few doubt that it is important. But, as noted in Chapter 1, the abyss between rich and poor has also increased in many countries that have experienced heavy foreign investment and a rising gross national product. Brazil is a key example. While few would desire slow growth or heavily restricted capital, increased productivity has not, of itself, resolved inequities in distribution of income. Yet many view lack of such productivity as the major cause of poverty.

A fourth view stresses cultural factors. The cultural habits of poor nations, the theory goes, are backward in the sense that they do not fit the requirements of modernization. Those requirements are a planning and organizational mentality, a drive to "get ahead" and the presence of the work ethic in some form, willingness to live life by the clock, a receptivity to modern science and technology, and a high level of educational skills. If the requirements imposed by a technological and industrial society are not accepted, poverty results, since the chief generator of wealth in the modern world is industrialization.

These four views are not exclusive of one another. But the analyses and emphases are different enough to evoke different responses. The response to a diagnosis of neo-colonialism as the problem is to call for major institutional changes in the rich countries, and within the rich sectors of poor countries. The response to cultural backwardness focuses almost entirely on certain sectors of poor countries, the "marginal" sectors.

These and other views have been aired in several important international meetings since 1974. A call has gone out for a New International Economic Order (NIEO). The proposals cluster in six areas, all aimed at decreasing the north/south gap.

1. Facilitating trade, with better terms of exchange for poor countries.

2. Increasing the Third World's share of industrial production.

3. Increasing the flow of capital—private investment and governmental aid—from rich to poor countries.

4. Relieving the debt burden of poor nations.

5. Increasing food production within poor countries.

6. Increasing the transfer of technology to poor countries.

With these proposals the poor countries are not calling for massive redistribution of wealth. They are not even seeking equality of income. Rather, they are asking that future opportunities for economic growth be restructured. The call is for equality of opportunity, rather than equality of outcome. And that, as Michael Harrington notes, is a classical capitalist concept, even when made by socialist nations, as many poor nations are.[6]

The poor countries have found little support among the major rich countries for the NIEO demands. Despite the lack of movement in international negotiations, some of the poor nations have embarked on highly imaginative strategies of their own for eradicating poverty, ignorance, and disease. One of these nations is Tanzania, whose president is quoted at the opening of this chapter.

In Tanzania the focus is on rural development, the achieving of self-reliant villages by labor-intensive means, using local resources, the chief of which is poor people themselves. That is a path far different from the dominant one in rich and poor worlds alike: the path of energy-intensive and capital-intensive industrialization, urbanization, and heavy reliance on international trade.

Yet, as Nyerere is the first to admit, a new path, such as Tanzania's, still requires international assistance and trade —and the recognition that ours is One World. The conclusion is this: whatever their efforts, the poor nations are, and remain, dependent on the rich for the eradication of poverty. For better or worse, for richer or poorer, it is one house.

STUDY PROJECT

This study project has two purposes: 1) to comprehend some of the dynamics between rich nations and poor; 2) to formulate a response on the basis of what has been uncovered.

A. Imagine joining friends for coffee and chocolate pastries. What is known about coffee and the coffee trade, about cocoa and the chocolate industry? On newsprint or a blackboard, write your analysis of various factors. The following questions may organize the discussion:

1. Who produces the coffee/cocoa, for whom, by what means, and for what wages?

2. Where and how are they financed, transported, processed, marketed?

3. What are the trade regulations on importing and exporting of the two?

4. Who benefits most and who benefits least along the way from production of raw material to final consumer purchase?

5. What are the various interests and perspectives? For example, the Colombian peasant or Ghanaian plantation worker, the growers (landowners), the processors, transporters, grocers, the people drinking coffee and eating cake.

6. To conclude the discussion, ask: Are there any patterns that would shed light on these questions: Why do the poor stay poor? Why do the rich get richer?

Some other product that involves the lives of rich and poor might be chosen: bauxite for aluminum, bananas, rubber.

B. In testimony before Congress, the Interreligious Task Force on Food Policy included a statement of four controlling moral convictions:

First, the magnitude and persistence of crying human need ought to haunt all of us.

Second, much of this misery is needless, despite the limits to growth, the scarcity of some natural resources, and the finitude of the human family.

Third, because much of today's human misery is needless, it is morally intolerable.

Fourth, because our nation has a tremendous capacity to change this morally intolerable situation, it has a moral obligation to do so.[7]

The task force acknowledged that the U.S. cannot do everything and that many of the key decisions are internal to the nations involved. But it went on to say that human misery does call for American responses within the limits of the possible.

Accepting the four convictions above as a fair statement of a Christian perspective, the question becomes: What concretely should and can be done? What is your answer to that question? And of the things that can be done, of which might you be a part?

7

grave doubts
about growth

If it is agreed that economic output is a good thing, it follows by definition that there is not enough of it.
> —The President's Council of Economic Advisors' Economic Report of the President, 1971

Man has probably always worried about the environment because he was once totally dependent on it.
> —Anthony C. Fisher and Frederick M. Peterson "The Environment in Economics"

The Council of Economic Advisors evidently believe it is impossible to have too much of a good thing. Herman Daly responds: By that logic, "If rain is a good thing, a torrential downpour is, by definition, better!" [1]

Most American economists, probably most Americans, have assumed that a rising per capita gross national product makes us "better off." It's a "good thing," and we cannot get too much of it.

Now that is being contested. English economist Fred

Hirsch says that, on economic grounds alone, the wisdom of ever-increasing growth is subject to grave doubt. He makes his point by distinguishing two kinds of goods.

Some abundant goods can be enjoyed by all who have them. Thus, a good meal at my house doesn't detract from the pleasures my neighbors have at theirs. Some other goods, however, can be enjoyed only when there is some limit on their use. So it is with automobiles, for example. The pleasures of the automobile are real—until too many occupy the same roads or compete for the same parking spaces or join the same gasoline lines. The pleasures of a house with a view are likewise real—but only if not too many houses occupy the same area. If they do, the view from each house is likely to be that of other houses.

The advantage of holding some kinds of goods, says Hirsch, disappears when too many people have too much. The analogy, he says, is like standing on tiptoe in a crowd. If a few do it, there's a clear advantage. If all do, the advantage is lost.

There is, then, what we may call a "saturation threshold" in societies of high production and consumption. The crossing of this threshold means that the quality of life actually decreases with increased material abundance.[2]

Most of the world need not worry that affluence may be destructive of human well-being. But it is a real threat in some places—like North America or northern Europe. Warnings about wealth are also sounded in both Testaments—indeed, in the scriptures of all the world's great religions.

LIMITS TO GROWTH

Warnings today come from other quarters as well. Probably the most important is the varied assembly gathered around the "limits to growth" thesis. The basic premise is simple: unlimited material growth is not possible in a finite world. That has always been the case, of course. Yet only recently has there been genuine and widespread alarm about encroaching limits. Why? Because several major factors interact in such a way that an increase in any one of them worsens the situation for all. And of late all the factors have been on the increase.

There has been escalating depletion of vital but nonrenewable resources, at the same time that environmental deterioration has taken place on a vast scale, at the same time that population growth has reached historically explosive levels (though the rate of growth is now slowing significantly), at the same time that large affluent sectors have demanded and consumed more of almost everything. A planet suddenly grown rather small and exhibiting its fragility cannot sustain such trends. Something has to give, say the "limits to growth" prophets.

There are several deep-seated problems here. One is our basic perception of who we are and where we fit in the scheme of things. Note carefully the second quotation at the beginning of this chapter. To that it must be said not only that humans have always worried about their environment, but that our total dependence on the environment is not ended, and never can be.

Somehow over recent centuries we Westerners have lost the sense of belonging to the rest of nature. At the same time our powers to exploit it have multiplied enormously. This no doubt fed the illusion of having unlimited powers in a setting of unlimited resources. In any event, built-in limits were unacknowledged or largely ignored until recently, when we have had to relearn some old laws:

"Everything goes somewhere, but nothing ever goes away."

"There's no such thing as a free lunch."

"You can never do merely one thing."

If those who worry about the limits to growth are any-where near the truth, some important economic implica-tions follow. For richer nations, the economic goal should be changed from ever-increasing production and con-sumption to managing a relatively fixed stock of physical wealth. With that the aim of production would be to produce goods of high durability, made from recyclable materials, using renewable sources of energy.

This does not mean an end to economic growth. It does not even mean an end to increased material levels in some quarters—in the poorer nations, for example, where it is imperative. It does mean that the system would be treated as a dynamic, but enclosed, reality. The image is that of the planet as a spaceship.

BASIC CHALLENGES

If the limits-to-growth students are at all accurate, we face several basic challenges:

1. The basic strategy for solving social problems and closing the rich/poor gap would need drastic revision. Past strategy has been to bake ever bigger pies, rather than to slice differently pies of relatively fixed size. The answer has been, "more, ever more," so that the well-off could remain well-off, without need of sacrifice, while the poor could eventually join the ranks of a growing middle class. If the ever-bigger-pie strategy is frustrated by the interplay of resource, environmental, and economic limits, then we are shoved nearer an older and brutal equation: that one person's wealth is another's poverty, that riches held are riches withheld. We thought unending industrial ex-pansion had transcended that equation. If it has not, we are cast back, as Charles West says, "with the problems

of distributive justice, unmitigated by the illusion that human avarice can be reconciled with social equality by the infinite expansion of human productivity." [3]

The depth of the challenge to the way we Americans have solved social problems (by economic expansion) can hardly be overstated. Here Reinhold Niebuhr's insight of two decades ago is still so fresh it merits quotation in full.

> For it is certainly the character of our particular democracy, founded on a vast continent, expanding as a culture with its expanding frontier and creating new frontiers of opportunity when the old geographic frontiers were ended, that every ethical and social problem is solved by so enlarging the privileges that either an equitable distribution is made easier, or a lack of equity is rendered less noticeable. For in this abundance the least privileged members of the community are still privileged, compared with less favored communities. No democratic community has followed this technique of social adjustment more consistently than we. No other community had the resources to do so. . . .
>
> Yet the price which American culture has paid for this amelioration of social tensions through constantly expanding production has been considerable. It has created moral illusions about the ease with which the adjustment of interests to interests can be made in human society. These have imparted a quality of senti-

> mentality to both our religious and our secular, social, and political theories. It has also created a culture which regards the perfection of techniques as the guarantor of every cultural as well as of every social-moral value.[4]

2. Many widespread economic practices would need to be altered. By and large we have not put the premium on goods of high durability, made from recyclable materials, using renewable energy sources. Nor have we shifted the economic aim from increasing production and maximizing consumption to efficiently maintaining and distributing a relatively fixed stock of physical wealth. It takes little imagination to recognize that changes of Himalayan magnitude are called for if the limits-to-growth people are right.

3. The ranks are swelling of those who claim the challenge is not only to basic social strategy and common economic practices, but to ongoing existence itself. In much of the literature and many a conversation, the term used more and more is "sustainability." That is, can the good earth continue to provide, for both the nearer and farther future, if the gargantuan appetites of industrial societies persist? In J. Philip Wogaman's treatment of "economic conservationism" (the point of view reflected in this chapter) the alternative is put this way:

> Economic conservationism thus seeks to illuminate a crucial choice confronting the late 20th century world: Either we must drastically limit our production and consumption for the sake of an unlimited human future, or we shall have a limited future for the sake of unlimited present economic activity.[5]

Changing basic social strategy, altering common economic practices, fashioning a sustainable society itself—these are indeed fundamental challenges. If we add to them our earlier worry about a decrease in the quality of life in "overabundant" societies, we recognize the validity of today's grave doubts. Alarmist and doomsaying responses are probably not helpful; frequently they foster more paralysis than change. Yet equally unhelpful is the response, "Take it easy; something will turn up." Something may not. Or what does may not contribute to the conditions needed for a humane existence.

Deep down, the question soon becomes a religious one: what gives us hope and courage to embark upon a necessarily uncertain journey, and what provides nourishment along the way?

STUDY PROJECT

In *A Theory of Justice,* John Rawls conducts a thought experiment along these lines: A group of people is to create a just society from scratch. But a certain "veil of ignorance" is present. The members cannot know in advance what place they will have in the new society. The task then is to arrange the society's rules, responsibilities, and rewards in a manner that safeguards the basic interests of all. Put differently, the task is to assure that society's benefits and burdens are borne fairly.

You have a task similar to that assigned by Rawls. The following limitations pertain, however. 1) Only the economic arrangements, not all societal forms, are to be sketched in broad outline. 2) A community of only 5000 people is to be served by your model. It can be assumed the community has adequate, though not unlimited, material resources and skills.

1. What would be the primary characteristics of such

an economic system? (You are reminded that members cannot know in advance the place they will occupy in the town's economy.)

2. Using the community's newly planned economy as a tentative standard, how does the economy you know in real life measure up? More pointedly, how does it measure up in light of the issues raised in the chapters "Rich and Poor" and "Grave Doubts About Growth"? What changes are now called for, in either the real-life economy or your newly designed one?

3. Did Christian perspectives enter your planning of the new economy? What were these, and which were most important?

If you need help in arranging the economic rules and responsibilities, remember that a fundamental question of economics is: Who shall produce what and for whom? In sketching the economic arrangements it may help to follow these steps:

1. What products and services does your society need?

2. Who will produce them?

3. If each individual is not self-sufficient, then how will goods and services be traded?

4. Who will perform this function and at what price?

5. Can everyone in your society produce or are some too young, too old, too infirm or in some other way disabled? How are their needs met?

6. Is caring for these people an important service which will be rewarded?

7. Can everyone in your society produce equally well, or is there a diversity of talents and skills?

8. Will scarce talent be rewarded more than abundant talent?

8

gaining a christian perspective

Give us this day our daily bread.

—Matthew 6:11

Man shall not live by bread alone, but by every word that proceeds from the mouth of God.

—Matthew 4:4

For you know the grace of our Lord Jesus Christ, that though he was rich, yet for your sake he became poor, so that by his poverty you might become rich.

—2 Corinthians 8:9

[There is no Christian economic system.] Each time an unqualified religious sanction has been given—the church's investment in the feudal order, for example, or Protestant championing of laissez-faire capitalism—voices within the Christian faith have criticized the sanction. The prophets have not always been honored in the process, but they have always been present, calling for some critical distance from affirmation of any one economic system.

We should not be surprised that there is no Christian economics. The Christian ethic has always pointed to the Kingdom of God as the judging standard. And in light of that, no human institution ever warrants an unqualified benediction. We are sinners, and our economic life always shows it.

At the same time, Christianity has persistently endeavored to relate the faith to economic life, and to do so in an affirmative as well as critical manner. That is no surprise, either. For when it is whole, Christian faith seeks to penetrate the entire web of human existence, and economic life is one of the strands that runs throughout.

Can we offer some Christian perspectives for judging and shaping economic life? The task is necessarily modest, for even when we see most clearly, it is still "through a glass darkly." We are all too subject to skewed vision and errors of human judgment. And public life today is complex and confused. Nonetheless, seeing economic life in Christian perspective is incumbent upon us, if faith and life are to be of a piece. Let us then sketch five ideas.

1. ENOUGH IS BEST

All the great religious faiths, Christianity included, share some important economic content. All teach that the truly abundant life is one of self-discipline and a restraint upon the multiplication of material desires. Indeed, a joyful existence, they contend, is frustrated by unrestricted material indulgence. Contrary to the expectations of many, high indulgence corrupts and deadens rather than liberates and enlivens. "Enough is best," rather than "more is better," is the succinct way to say it.

But what is enough? The outer boundaries, at least, are clear. Real poverty is not enough. It kills the spirit and debilitates the body. It beats people down before they can walk even half tall. It brutalizes cell and soul alike. An economy that has the resources to meet basic human needs—food, shelter, clothing, health care, work, festivity—and does not meet them, fails the test. And any economy that simultaneously generates debilitating poverty in some quarters and unrestrained consumption in others has failed doubly.

Instead of "Can't Get Enough of that Wonderful Stuff," [1] the Wisdom Tradition states:

> Give me neither poverty nor riches;
> feed me with the food that is needful for
> me,
> lest I be full, and deny thee,
> and say, "Who is the Lord?"
> or lest I be poor and steal,
> and profane the name of my God.
> (Proverbs 30:8-9).

Material sufficiency is not its own end, however. For Christian faith it is a means to other ends: the fostering of human community, the cultivation of mind and spirit, the celebration of creation, the enjoyment of communion with God. All of these are rendered more difficult if poverty strangles life. At the same time, they have nonmaterial dimensions. So material well-being cannot, of itself, realize human fulfillment.

Herman Daly speculates that community may in fact require some degree of scarcity, "without which cooperation, sharing and friendship would have no organic reason to be." [2] Many studies of affluent neighborhoods reveal two realities: materially self-sufficient households, and those diseases which signal the lack of healthy human community (extensive drug use, high divorce and suicide rates, loneliness and depression). Having "everything" seems to suffocate human interdependence. Philip Slater writes:

> It is easy to produce examples of the many ways in which Americans attempt to minimize, circumvent, or deny the interdependence upon which all human societies are based. We seek a private house, a private means of transportation, a private garden, a private laundry, self-service stores, and do-it-yourself skills of every kind. An enormous technology seems to have set itself the task of making it unnecessary for one human being ever to ask anything of another in the course of going about his daily business. Even within the family Americans are unique in their feeling that each member should have a separate room, and even a separate telephone, television, and car, when economically possible. We seek more and more privacy, and feel more and more alienated and lonely when we get it. What accidental contacts we do have, furthermore, seem more intrusive, not only because they are unsought but because they are unconnected with any familiar pattern of interdependence.[3]

2. STEWARD AND NEIGHBOR

"Who is my neighbor?" and "Am I my neighbor's keeper?" are basic questions for Christian faith. They are also basic questions for economic life. H. Richard Niebuhr eloquently states the Christian perspective:

Who, finally, is my neighbor, the com-
panion whom I have been commanded
to love as myself? . . . He is the near one
and the far one; the one removed from
me by distances in time and space, in
convictions and loyalties. . . . The neighbor is in past and present and future, yet
he is not simply mankind in its totality
but rather in its articulation, the community of individuals in community. He is
Augustine in the Roman Catholic Church
and Socrates in Athens, and the Russian
people, and the unborn generations who
will bear the consequences of our failures, future persons for whom we are ad-
ministering the entrusted wealth of nature
and other greater common gifts. He is man
and he is angel and he is animal and inorganic being, all that participates in being.[4]

In the economics of the house the householder is
steward for all creation in a community that extends to
both past and future generations. The neighbor is "all that
participates in being." In Christian perspective, the lines
of responsible relationship extend that far.

The Genesis creation story describes the steward's
responsibility with a word, *dominion*. We are to "have
dominion" over all things. But how is dominion exercised? And what does this mandate mean for economic
life?

Christians will answer that by letting Jesus Christ define dominion. The earliest Christian confession is that
"Jesus is Lord" *(dominus)*. He has dominion over all
things. He is also confessed as "true humanity," thus
showing us how we are to be genuinely human.

The question then becomes, how does true humanity exercise dominion? For Christians the answer is found by looking to the nature of Jesus' lordship. Here we can only underscore some key words that characterize Jesus' lordship. The lordship of Jesus is a caring dominion, exercised in gratitude, steeped in the sense of the pervasive presence of God, and carried out in the knowledge that all life is a gift from God.

This caring entails suffering. It is suffering for the sake of bringing wholeness to all things, wholeness that has been broken by sin. Part of this is "being articulate for others" (as Douglas Hall defines *stewardship*), including the nonhuman neighbor.[5]

Perhaps it is helpful to say what proper dominion is not. It is not a power-driven mastery over nature and society. This is the corruption of dominion. This is domination. And this is the "lording it over" which Satan offered Jesus and which Jesus rejected in the wilderness temptation (Matthew 4). Instead, Jesus chooses the kind of dominion so beautifully captured in Isaiah's picture of the suffering servant:

> Behold my servant, whom I uphold,
> my chosen, in whom my soul delights;
>
> I have put my Spirit upon him,
> he will bring forth justice to the nations.
>
> He will not cry or lift up his voice,
> or make it heard in the street;
>
> a bruised reed he will not break,
> and a dimly burning wick he will not
>   quench;
> he will faithfully bring forth justice.

He will not fail or be discouraged
till he has established justice in the earth;
and the coastlands wait for his law.
(Isa. 42:1-4)

Here are the great religious virtues that define dominion—humility, restraint, reverence, gratitude, and the
striving for justice. Jesus' lordship exhibits just such
traits as the traits of "true humanity."

But what does such dominion have to do with economic life?

One reply is to note the contrast with the economic
life we know best. There has been little hesitation about
breaking "a bruised reed" or quenching "a dimly burn-
ing wick." The mindset has been one of conquest and control, of mastery and unlimited intervention. A well-known
American social scientist exhibits just this orientation:

> Deliberate control [of human genes]
> would soon benefit science and technol-
> ogy, which in turn would facilitate further
> hereditary improvement, which again
> would extend science, and so on in a self-
> reinforcing spiral without limit. In other
> words, when man has conquered his
> own biological evolution, he will have
> laid the basis for conquering everything
> else. The universe will be his at last.[6]

If this is the ruling disposition—"conquering everything, the universe will be his at last"—it is small wonder
our technology exhibits little of humility or limits, and
almost nothing of awe or reverence before the mystery
of life and the universe. There is nothing here of the
knowledge of humans as fallible creatures, co-siblings
with the rest of creation, ultimately dependent on their

Creator for the fragile breath of life. Nor is there much basis for a neighbor-love that is stewarding rather than conquering, nurturing rather than controlling, suffering-with rather than lording-over.

Unfortunately, for all its benefits, our economic life has reflected these broad cultural orientations. It has been rapacious and short-sighted, brutal toward nonhuman nature, unmindful of future generations. Whatever else we may say, a Christian notion of stewardship and dominion would ask that the drive of highly productive industrialized economies be rendered more gentle and generous toward "all that participates in being."

3. UNIVERSALITY AND EQUALITY

Another Christian perspective that gives expression to our hopes is the strong thrust toward universality and equality. The root conviction here is that all human beings are equally the objects of God's unbounded love and thus, "in that which is most basic . . . the value of each life, we are all equal." [7]

Precisely what this universality and equality mean for economic life will vary by time and place. But a broad, well-defined line can be sketched: no human group should be excluded from a reasonable share of the benefits of an economy, nor should any be exempted from shouldering a reasonable share of the burdens. "A reasonable share" is, of course, notoriously vague. But it is far from meaningless to insist that all be included in a fair sharing of both benefits and burdens.

Perhaps more precision can be given by beginning with the idea of an equal sharing of benefits and burdens, and then going on to say that economic inequalities are justified only if they can be shown to serve the common good (instead of private interests only). [8]

4. HUMAN SIN

The sober Christian teaching about human sinfulness has implications for economic life. This teaching says that individual and collective self-centeredness operates persistently at levels both conscious and unconscious, and that people organize their lives, personally and in groups, to serve their own well-being at the expense of the well-being of others. The theological term "original sin" is a way of pointing to the pervasiveness and stubbornness of this perverse self-centeredness. No human achievement, however grand and good, escapes it.

For economic life there is a clear implication: a wise economic order guards against unchecked concentrations of power and minimizes opportunities for the selfish uses of power. We should be suspicious of powerful groups which justify economic privilege on the promise that it will be exercised "in the best interests of all." This is not to say there may not be genuinely sincere and benevolent persons among such groups. It is only to say that they are also sinners, and that evil arises from maldistribution of power, even that exercised by "good" people. And sin affects not only private centers of power, but also government planners and regulators.

We cannot rule out occasional, justified, high concentrations of economic power. They may be called for as the best of clearly imperfect social arrangements: to build a large public transportation network, for example, or a needed dam and irrigation project, to keep a postal system working, to address large-scale emergency needs, or to provide public education for masses of people. But the teaching on sin warns that such concentrations, whether in public or private hands, require special justification, and that a wise system has built-in checks upon even the necessary amassing of economic power.

5. LIMITS AND SERENITY

The folk wisdom, "Money can't buy happiness," is wiser than we give it credit. Human appetites and expectations are nearly insatiable. They outstrip our achievements more frequently than not.

We Americans have invested economic life with high expectations. In the past few decades, at least, we have tied much of "the pursuit of happiness" to it. Our successes as a great commercial nation have reinforced this.

But "happiness" is an elusive reality, consisting of as many nonmaterial dimensions as material ones. In any event, economic life can supply only some of its ingredients; and while they are crucial ones, they are far fewer than a consumerist mentality assumes.

The root error is not with economic life as such. The error is a failure to recognize limits in life and a failure to achieve a certain acceptance of them. Economic life cannot yield the full measure of well-being because it cannot overcome the fragmentary character of human existence. It can produce much, but it cannot produce the harmony and wholeness that broken life in a fractured history knows only in fleeting and fragile and partial ways. The world of economic life, itself restless and troubled, cannot yield what even life at its best does not.

There *is* the possibility of living with limits and finding serenity within them. But it requires a vision of the whole that day-to-day living cannot on its own evidence fully validate. It requires a courageous belief about the true, the good, and the beautiful that no immediate experience can wholly verify. It requires the confidence of faith, a trust in the reality of another kingdom, a kingdom of God. We ask too much of economic life, even economic life at its most vigorous, when we ask of it a full measure of happiness and a sure path to social peace. Those are promised only by gods of our own making.

So our five guides from Christian faith for economic life are:

1. A notion of material sufficiency or "enough" (in contrast to unlimited production and maximum consumption).

2. An understanding of stewardship and dominion as gentle caring extended to all of creation (in contrast to a "species chauvinism" on the part of humans, and a sense of time that takes in only the current generation).

3. An understanding of universality and equality as important base lines for an economic order (in contrast to exclusion of particular human groups from either benefits or burdens of economic life).

4. An understanding that human sinfulness calls for checks against large aggregations of economic power (because of the human propensity to use power in narrowly self-interested ways).

5. An understanding of *inherent limits* in life that tempers our culture's high expectations of economic life.

These are only broad considerations, but they are important because it is the broad baselines that give an economic order its essential character. The baselines are also the points where a people's faith and morality most deeply touch economic life.

It is tempting to stop here. But we cannot. For we have yet to come full face toward the center of Christian faith, Jesus Christ. Mohandas Gandhi, though not a Christian, often had a keener eye for Jesus than those of us who are. In 1915 he was asked to address a gathering of Indian economists. He chose what must have seemed to them a curious subject, Jesus. He said:

> "It is easier for a camel to go through the eye of a needle than for a rich man to enter into the kingdom of God!" Here

you have an eternal rule of life stated in the noblest words the English language is capable of producing. But the disciples nodded unbelief as we do even to this day. . . . I hold that economic progress . . . is antagonistic to real progress. Hence the ancient ideal has been the limitation of activities promoting wealth. This does not put an end to all material ambition. . . . But we have always recognized that it is a fall from the ideal. It is a beautiful thing to know that the wealthiest among us have often felt that to have remained voluntarily poor would have been a higher state.[9]

One doubts that the wealthier of the economists present left, divested themselves of property, and happily embraced voluntary poverty! At the same time, many no doubt heard the ring of truth in what Gandhi said. It is a fascinating fact that in so many traditions, Christianity included, "the wealthiest . . . have often felt that to have remained voluntarily poor would have been a higher state." We just don't associate saints with riches, except in the divesting of them on the path toward riches of a different order.

What are Christians to make of Jesus' poverty? Or his instructions to the disciples to travel light, without money, and adopt the life-style of the wandering poor (Mark 6:7-13)? What do we make of the economics of the earliest church, holding "all things in common," selling possessions and goods and distributing "to each, as any had need" (Acts 2:44-45; 4:34-35)? Were such actions a consequence of the faith itself, and central to it? Or only marginal, one possibility among many?

Is Paul's language for the work of Christ, in 2 Cor. 8:9, only "spiritual"? And is it in fact, harder for the rich to enter God's kingdom than for a camel to pass through the needle's eye? Can one, indeed, thread a needle with a camel?

What is clear is that in matters economic, as in others, Jesus turns the tables. The way of the cross is something other than our existing human expectations and the well-traversed economic path. If in political life the way of the cross is an alternative to both insurrection and quietism, in economic matters perhaps it is voluntary poverty, an alternative to both the way of the rich and the way of the involuntarily poor.

In any event, we cannot avoid the question: What does the way of the cross mean for the followers of Jesus in the economic order in which they find themselves? The final chapter seeks to take this question seriously.

STUDY PROJECT

1. Mark Twain once quipped, "It's not the parts of the Bible I don't understand that bother me, but those I do." This is a healthy reminder not to hedge on, or rationalize, the hard sayings. But there is also a great deal of the Bible we aren't acquainted with. Readers may wish to explore some or all of the following texts. Newer commentaries should be consulted, since recent biblical scholarship has greatly enhanced our knowledge of the social, political, and economic world of these texts.

> Isaiah 58
> Deuteronomy 15:1-15
> Leviticus 25
> Luke 4:16-21
> Luke 6:17-36

Matthew 25:31-46
Acts 2:37-47; 4:32-35
Mark 6:7-13
2 Corinthians 8:1-15

What meanings, including economic, does each text have in its own setting? What meanings would you draw for our setting?

2. Eating bread may be a material and individual act, but breaking it and sharing it is a spiritual one as well. The sacrament of the Eucharist symbolizes, in the breaking of bread, the breaking and sharing of Christ for all creation. It also symbolizes a new way of living, though this has been too little emphasized in our understanding of the Lord's Supper. Francine Cardman has rightly noted that the Eucharist is to be understood in light of Jesus' post-resurrection breaking of bread with the disciples, as well as in view of their last supper together. Then "eating and drinking with the Risen Jesus [becomes] a new way of living in the world, and that new way is almost limitless in its social, political, and economic implications. For the Eucharist to remain only inward or spiritual is to blaspheme the sacrament."[10]

Some readers may wish to explore the "social, political, and economic implications" of the sacrament and share findings with the larger group. Two books of help are the following: Monica Hellwig, *The Eucharist and the Hunger of the World*, Paulist, 1976, and Gustave Martelet, *The Risen Christ and the Eucharistic World*, Seabury, 1976. The former is short and highly readable. The latter is longer and more technical, though very rich.

Martelet includes this passage:

To involve human food and drink symbolically in a meal of love implies at the very least that in real life we have done nothing to deprive others of them; and, even further, that we are doing or have done . . . everything that is humanly and Christianly necessary and possible to ensure that these elementary supplies are produced in sufficient quantity and shared equitably. If this were not done, to take the bread and wine and offer them to the Lord would become intolerably false, since we would be seeking to give God with one hand what we were unjustly withholding from men with the other.[11]

3. This chapter began with the sentence, "There is no Christian economic system." That means that no single way of organizing our economic life will measure up to the standards which the kingdom of God upholds. Until full justice reigns, economic life will need reform. Yet we have ended this chapter with a question: Are more rigorous standards expected of the followers of Jesus than those which can reasonably be expected from society at large? As Kierkegaard reminds us, society has a great many admirers of Jesus, but few disciples. Discipleship is a far more exacting vocation with a more exacting ethic.

Through the centuries the church has consistently answered *yes* to the question above, even when the performance of believers has consistently fallen short. Yet in America the church has, with few exceptions, given little thought to what a more demanding ethic for economic life might mean. We have not often asked what the way of the cross means concretely in matters of "daily bread."

What do you think should be the economic ethic of the

churches in America today? What does discipleship mean in current economic life?

The question requires time for struggle, and the results might profitably be shared with a study group. It might help to consult a short and lively book on the subject: John V. Taylor, *Enough Is Enough,* Augsburg, 1977; it includes a study guide.

9

the church and the 1980s

A God without wrath brought men without sin into a kingdom without judgment through the ministrations of a Christ without a cross.

—H. Richard Niebuhr,
The Kingdom of God in America, 1937

This was H. Richard Niebuhr's characterization of Protestant liberalism. It was Christian ethics without tears, a theology of optimism in "an officially optimistic society." [1]

Even the religious traditions that did preach a God of wrath, a kingdom of judgment, and a Christ with a cross —such as the revivalist traditions—shared the official optimism of American *economic* life. And since America's business was business, the economic optimism easily modulated to that of a general cultural confidence in an unbounded future.

Such confidence is now gone. Whether it will return is a question not likely to be answered in the '80s, at least not in the affirmative.

If we are in a period of baffling, precarious economic transition, then it is also a time of necessary experimentation, risky though that be. All signs are that the experimentation is on a grand scale, and much of it is involuntary!

In a transition time, some communities serve as *anticipatory communities*. They work out, in nuts-and-bolts fashion, new patterns of life more appropriate to an emerging epoch. They give present form to a hoped-for future, thereby showing that what might someday be undertaken on a larger scale has already found a recognizable incarnation.[2]

A highly pluralist nation, with myriad conflicting interests, both domestic and international, has great difficulty being a cohesive anticipatory community. Of course, government must play a major role in fashioning any new economic order; public policy is simply indispensible to our life together. But there are other communities as well, and in a time inherently unstable they are often the more creative ones.

It is an open question whether portions of the Christian church in the United States might be such communities. It may be that Christianity is so acculturated, so entangled in the American economic success story, that it will respond no differently to the harsh realities of an in-between time than the culture as a whole. Douglas John Hall may be right in saying that Christianity has been "the official religion of the officially optimistic society."[3] As such, it stands as much in need of "conversion" as does the culture at large.

But there is a long tradition of dreaming in the great religions, and sometimes that utopian impulse has itself been a factor in "conversion." It has helped effect a new way of seeing life, thinking about it, and living it out. Moreover, there are already intimations of hopeful anticipatory communities to be found in "real life." The following images of the church for the '80s are drawn from them. As importantly, they are drawn from Israel and the early church, though the language here is not traditional.

1. DATES, NOT PUMPKINS

The church should be a community of dates instead of pumpkins.[4] For Americans there will be tremendous pressures to meet short-term economic goals, and many, perhaps most, will be pursued at the expense of future generations and the present poor. How and where will we get more energy? How do we get the economy rolling again? Doesn't the poor nations' call for the New International Economic Order mean more American unemployment?

When the choices become fewer and the constraints more numerous, and so many pressures are focused on the short haul, where is the community that dreams grander dreams and plants dates instead of pumpkins? Pumpkins you can harvest in six months, dates have to be planted and tended by people who will not live to harvest them. Dates are for future generations. Pumpkins, no doubt, will be planted in abundance by Americans confronting a tightening future. Dates will not. It's a Jeremiah time, and like him the church should settle in for the longer stretch.

2. ENOUGH IS ENOUGH

The church in its affluent sectors should be a "goodbye, more; hello, less" church,[5] a community of "enough is enough."[6] The appetite of rich industrial nations is gargantuan. And those nations, including the United States, will try to corner whatever is needed to feed that appetite. Almost no one expects this decade to see a happy closing of the poor/rich abyss, either within most nations or between them. Rather, within rich sectors, we will likely see more of the defense found with increased frequency in public media, often sponsored by the giant corporations and commercial interest groups. One Mobil Corporation ad tells the fable, "Why Elephants Can't Live on Peanuts." The smaller "have-not animals" all rebuke an elephant for her mammoth appetite and enormous consumption. They then deny access to her feeding grounds. But soon they, too, are in serious trouble because they themselves cannot do the necessary heavy work the elephant does. "Help, help," the have-not animals shout. "Crisis, crisis." The elephant comes to their aid and passes along the moral:

"You see, . . . you need a big beast for a big job, and a big beast has big needs. Not just to stay alive and growing, but to put aside for tomorrow. And to have a bit extra for working especially hard, or for sharing with have-not animals." [7]

Where, in the midst of this defensiveness from the institutionalized affluent, is a community of "less is more," even a community of "enough is best"? Where is a community that might venture to celebrate relinquishment? The church in the '80s should help affluent people choose for themselves, or at least adjust to, a life of economic moderation.

This would be done in the hope that elsewhere, among the genuinely poor, it might be "goodbye, less; hello, more." That is not likely to happen on any large scale in this decade; yet, like dates, the seeds should be planted now. And though the early church lived in a quite different economic order than we, the guiding notion Paul commended is not outdated: "I do not mean that others should be eased and you burdened, but that as a matter of equality your abundance at the present time should supply their want, . . . that there may be equality" (2 Cor. 8:13-14).[8]

3. VICTORIA, NOT BAGDAD

The church should be a "Victoria and not Bagdad" community. The '80s will be a convulsive decade in economic life. In the midst of this, the church needs to affirm every ordinary good thing it can, from old traditions that still hold us together to a prayer of thanks that the sun didn't let us down but came up yet one more day. The church should celebrate the ordinary everyday triumphs of creation over chaos.

In G. K. Chesterton's *The Man Who Was Thursday* there is a vigorous debate between two poets, Mr. Gregory and Mr. Syme, about art. Mr. Gregory says "an artist is an anarchist" and "the poet delights in disorder only." He goes on to explain why "all the clerks and navvies in the railway trains looks so sad and tired, so very sad and tired."

> I will tell you [why]. It is because they know that the train is going right. It is because they know that whatever place they have taken a ticket for, that place they will reach. It is because after they have passed Sloane Square they know that the next station must be Victoria, and nothing but Victoria. Oh, their wild rapture! Oh, their eyes like stars and their souls again in Eden, if the next station were unaccountably Baker Street!

Syme answers this with equal conviction:

> It is you who are unpoetical. . . . If what you say of clerks is true, they can only be

as prosaic as your poetry. The rare, strange thing is to hit the mark; the gross, obvious thing is to miss it. We feel it is epical when man with one wild arrow strikes a distant bird. Is it not also epical when man with one wild engine strikes a distant station? Chaos is dull; because in chaos the train might indeed go anywhere, to Baker Street or to Bagdad. But man is a magician, and his whole magic is in this, that he does say Victoria, and lo! it is Victoria.

I tell you . . . that every time a train comes in I feel that it has broken past batteries of besiegers, and that man has won a battle against chaos. You say contemptuously that when one has left Sloane Square one must come to Victoria. I say that one might do a thousand things instead, and that whenever I really come there I have a sense of hairbreadth escape. And when I hear the guard shout out the word "Victoria" it is not an unmeaning word. . . . It is indeed "Victoria"; it is the victory of Adam.[9]

A "Victoria rather than Bagdad" community: in the '80s we should affirm all routine goodness, celebrate it and hold it high like the bread and wine of the sacrament.

This celebration intersects economic life because the material world is the "stuff" of God's creation—and redemption. One of the oldest theological themes, rooted in the Greek word *oikos*, (the world as a household) is "the divine economy." And a large part of its meaning is viewing the material world sacramentally, treating its common fare with reverence, and seeing its origin and destiny in God.

Alexander Schmemann, the Eastern Orthodox theologian, points in this direction when he comments on the sentence of the German philosopher, Feuerbach, that "man is what he eats."

> Man must eat in order to live; he must take the world into his body and transform it into himself, into flesh and blood. He is indeed that which he eats, and the whole world is presented as one all-embracing banquet table for man. And this image of the banquet remains throughout the whole Bible, the central image of life. It is the image of life at its creation and also the image of life at its end and fulfillment: " . . . that you eat and drink at my table in my kingdom." [10]

Granted that the meaning of "Victoria and not Bagdad" is not the full panorama pointed to by the phrase, "the divine economy." But there is this crucial task for the church in the '80s, to help evoke awe for the ordinary gifts of the material creation and for routine goodness itself, including the routine goodness for which economic life is responsible: food and table, work and reward, resources and their good use for human and nonhuman neighbors of the whole household.

4. SACRED STRANGER

The church might be—should be—a sacred stranger in secular society. Fifty years ago Howard Becker made an important study of secularization. He studied personality types in societies undergoing the kind of change that called into question the values and perspectives of the former order. Older understandings of the holy in particular seemed overturned, and the movement in such times seemed to be toward more secular patterns of freedom and openness. Becker found that in such settings some persons abandon all ties to older tradition in attempting to embrace the new. For them, whatever is new displaces the old. Others hold fast to the old and are often swept aside by the new, at least with respect to their influence in the social order. But those who exert the most creative leadership in such times are ones Becker calls "sacred strangers in secular society." The sacred stranger embraces the new possibilities, but in doing so does not abandon the values and meanings and insights of the old sacred order. Such a person recasts older understandings in new patterns. Indeed, the past provides some of the "stuff" of the new vision for the emerging order. This person is the sacred stranger in the midst of secular society, participating fully but not captured by the dominant culture.[11]

The church would, as sacred stranger, mine its own peculiar traditions with greater ardor; there would be more, not less, engagement with the lives of the saints and the ancient symbols and confessions; there would be a genuinely pious observation of the liturgical traditions and intense adherence to the rhythm of the church year. In the very midst of shaking foundations the tradition would be called on for the necessary recasting of a different future.

Part of this tradition is the vast range of societal arrangements by which the church has tried and is trying to relate the faith to economic life. We ignore much that is vital in history if we think only of Protestantism's affinity for capitalism or the church's underwriting of the feudal order. Likewise we cut ourselves off from resources if we overlook the experiments with economic life in the global church today. A sacred stranger in American economic life might look to these varied traditions, many of them small, for some clues in a time of economic experimentation and transition.

The church would be and should be a sacred *stranger*. We have entrapped ourselves in the American economic success story. ("The walls of gold entomb us," a hymn line has it.) Moving out of that entrapment will mean becoming a stranger to the larger society.

R. H. Tawney, writing in *Religion and the Rise of Capitalism*, has a sentence that might be a place to begin reflection:

> Compromise is as impossible between the Church of Christ and the idolatry of wealth, which is the practical religion of capitalist societies, as it was between the Church and the State idolatry of the Roman Empire.[12]

Walter Brueggemann takes his cues for reflection from biblical experience. When the Hebrews were in Egypt, their suffering gave them a perspective different from that of the "royal consciousness" of high Egyptian society. Royal consciousness expressed itself in an economics of concentrated wealth, a politics of oppression, and a religion of accessibility (the domestication of the gods). By contrast the Hebrews, from the Exodus event, moved toward an economics of equality, a politics of justice, and a religion of God's transcendent freedom.

We know the story from there. From early on the Israelites not only compromised their alternative; they even had their own version of the economies of concentrated wealth, the politics of oppression and, with the temple under Solomon, a religion of God's domestication.[13] It was civil religion, worshiping something akin to the golden calf rejected under Moses' leadership, although the God invoked to sanction this triangle of economics/politics/religion was the God of Abraham, Isaac, and Jacob.

Today, in a world where more for some frequently means less for others, an economics of affluence seems to result increasingly in a politics of oppression. And for many in affluent sectors there is a yearning for religious or quasi-religious sanction to cover such politics, often justified as "necessity" and occasionally even as destiny or mission.

Is there somewhere in this society a community that is a sacred stranger to it, *sacred* in its drawing upon a religious tradition that is not wholly acculturated, and *stranger* in that it offers the outlines of an economics of equality, a politics of justice, and a religion of God's freedom to do a new thing amidst the old, including a new thing in economic life?

5. THE NERVE OF FAILURE

The church should be a community that possesses "the nerve of failure." [14] One of the requisites for successfully negotiating a time of major economic transition is the presence of people who will risk for a future they will not likely see. They refuse to engage in what David Riesman calls "the lesser-evil thinking which poses immediate alternatives" and instead engage in that thinking "which confronts us with great hopes and great plans." [15] They dare to dream grander dreams even as the constraints multiply.

On the face of it, that appears "impractical." It certainly is a kind of foolishness, like planting dates instead of pumpkins. It is the route by which "success" requires a season of risking that will undoubtedly entail failure in a period of trial-and-error. In the process, we will discover some faults we didn't even know we had!

Such a community of the nerve of failure must live from a source it does not possess of itself. It must draw upon a power that transcends it and its immediate cultural setting. It requires a perspective like that of Reinhold Niebuhr:

> Nothing that is worth doing can be achieved in our lifetime; therefore we must be saved by hope. Nothing which is true or beautiful or good makes complete sense in any immediate context of history; therefore we must be saved by faith. Nothing we do, however virtuous, can be accomplished alone; therefore we are saved by love. No virtuous act is quite as virtuous from the standpoint of our friend or foe as it is from our standpoint. Therefore we must be saved by the final form of love which is forgiveness.[16]

LIVING BY MEMORY AND HOPE

In the 1980s the church, or at least portions of it, could be one of the anticipatory communities needed for a new economic life. It could be both local and global in a time when the whole human family is the basic unit of economic reality. It could be a community of "enough," of "Victoria," of dates, a sacred stranger venturing to risk in a precarious historical moment. It could live, even "abundantly," from memory and hope; from memory, because we have been all these places before—Egypt, Israel, Babylon, Rome, Constantinople—and were sustained; from hope, since we know the creative task is possible in that it has already happened—in dying and rising again.

Above all it could be a community that points to the *ground* of memory and hope. In that its trust is certain, even when we see the '80s only through a smoky glass. The church trusts in transformation because the possibility is God's, and for no other reason. But that is enough. For when "hope seemed hopeless," Abraham, contemplating his own body, "as good as dead," and knowing as well "the deadness of Sarah's womb," yet put his trust in God, the God "who makes the dead live and summons things that are not yet in existence as if they already were" (Rom. 4:17-21).[17]

STUDY PROJECT

Chapter 8 concluded with a question: What does the way of the cross mean for the followers of Jesus in the economic order in which they find themselves? Chapter 9 attempted the beginnings of a reply, doing so with some pictures of the kind of community the church might be and ought to be in the years ahead.

Two questions should be posed in order to pursue a more satisfying and complete response.

1. Are there other images of the church, not yet discussed, which you see as helpful toward an answer to the question of Chapter 8? What are they? How do they reflect the way of the cross?

2. What do you see as the *specific* economic implications suggested by the images discussed in this chapter? What are those of *your* picture(s) of the church? Are there economic steps you and others can take immediately? Are there others which require a longer term but which can find some beginnings, or some preparation, now? How do these steps reflect the way of the cross?

10

the
God-wrestle

All things by immortal power
    Near or far
    Hiddenly
To each other linkéd are,
That thou canst not stir a flower
Without troubling of a star.
          —Francis Thompson

We do not have historical precedents for the fundamental transformation of advanced industrial societies, either capitalist or socialist. Yet that basic transformation now appears in the making. Why? The causes are many and only a few can be addressed in these last pages. Yet the realities we do point to are critical for economic life. They also intersect Christian faith at profound levels.

Economics, we noted earlier, is management of the public household (oikos).[1] But the nature of this home management depends largely upon what a culture or historical era means by "home."[2] "Home" is the picture of reality we carry around in our heads, the constellation of basic understandings and images that inform our activity and underlie our institutions. A commonplace expression, "This is really *home* to me," means "I understand this world; I am part of it and it is part of me."

A two-way influence runs between economic life and people's sense of home. If the sense of home changes markedly, economic life will reflect the new life-orientation. When, for example, the Hebrews experienced the dramatic reality of Yahweh as liberator of the enslaved, their new covenant contained provision upon provision, detail upon detail, for economic life, an economic life in sharp contrast to the pattern of Egyptian society. And when the early Jewish-Christians responded to the new reality they met in Jesus, their economic life also took new form. Lands and houses were sold, goods were shared in common, provision was made for distribution according to need. A community that experiences some fundamental change in its guiding sense of reality comes eventually to reflect that change in its economic life.

Change is complex, however, and often the direction is from institutional change to change in the way we view ourselves and the world. Institutional patterns shape our sense of home. The Industrial Revolution, to cite but one example, has brought about changes everywhere that "modernity" has taken root, changes not only in economic organization but in people's values, habits of mind, and outlook.

What faces us now—the transformation of industrial society—is bound up with changes from *both* directions. As we have seen in earlier chapters, the patterns of economic life itself have been rendered doubtful. For this reason, there are now strong institutional imperatives for basic change. At the same time, many people have experienced a different "sense of home" taking hold, and they strain to find its expression in economic life. "Simplicity," "alternative life-style," "self-reliance," and "decentralization" are almost code words in a significant movement.

This chapter can address only some aspects of the transformation of industrial society. It will focus on the changing sense of home, and, within that, on our understanding
of the material world, our place in it, and economic life
as a reflection of these.

STORED SUN AND MASTERY

The New Testament word *oikos* is the root word not
only for "economics" but for "ecosystem" as well. The
ecosystem is the living skin of the planet, organic and
inorganic matter that is constantly in process in a set of
complex relationships. All economic life is totally dependent upon the ecosystem. Given that dependence, the
governing influences should flow from the biophysical
world to the economic world. Yet industrial society has
turned the relationship upside down; economics had dic-
tated the terms of treatment of the biophysical world,
rather than nature setting the basic terms for economic
life.

What permitted this inversion? A part of nature itself,
namely, the dominant energy sources that have fueled
industrial society as we know it. These sources are the
nonrenewables—oil, natural gas, coal, uranium. They are,
in effect, "stored sun" and have allowed us to "turn on"
and "turn off" the sun at will, bypassing the need to wait
upon cycles and seasons for much of economic life and
permitting us to construct an artificial nature of our own
design. With these energy sources we could have a world
of our own making. That has been the dream of both
capitalism and socialism.

In his prison notes of the 1940s Dietrich Bonhoeffer
wrote: "The aim: to be independent of nature. Nature
was formerly conquered by spiritual means, with us by

technical organization of all kinds. Our immediate environment is not nature, but organization." [3]

This technical conquest of nature, in order to be free of its limits, vagaries, and onslaughts, has permitted a whole way of viewing ourselves and the rest of creation. That we could have a world of our own making has quite literally "gone to our heads" and deeply shaped the way we see things, our sense of home. Our *minds* have been so changed that we view ourselves and the world differently, we understand differently, from hunter-gatherer societies, or agrarian societies of a preindustrial era. Our understanding is that we are the masters of nature and makers of history, indeed, the captains of our own souls. Nature is seen essentially as "resources" for our engineering projects; the world is the "stage" for the human drama.

There is a massive illusion here, "a crack in the cosmic egg." [4] It is that we are "independent of nature" and can circumvent the limits and requirements of the biophysical world or dictate the terms of human relationship to it.

The illusion is reflected in a quotation from an earlier chapter: "Man has probably always worried about the environment because he was once totally dependent on it." [5] We *are*, not *once were*, totally dependent upon the environment. What has transpired is not at all "independence from nature"; rather, *a part of nature*, indeed a nonrenewable part, has been used *for a different organization of economic life*. The basic dependence of the economic system upon the ecosystem has not been altered in the least, even when a number of what might be called "secondary dependencies" have been changed so that "organization" rather than "nature" has become the more *immediate* environment.

Yet even this is highly illusory, since *all* of the material aspects of organization—buildings, streets, power, transportation—are varied forms of *nature*. Our immediate environment is also nature.

Few economists have been so acutely aware of the relationship of economic system to ecosystem as has Kenneth Boulding, in part because of his deep Quaker sense for the larger mysteries of life. Many years ago he wrote:

> Economists in particular, for the most part, have failed to come to grips with the ultimate consequences of the transition from the open to the closed earth. . . . The closed earth of the future requires economic principles which are somewhat different from those of the open earth of the past. . . . The earth has become a single spaceship, without unlimited reservoirs of anything, either for extraction or for pollution, and in which, therefore, man must find his place in a cyclical ecological system.[6]

Still, even this can be misleading, given the dominant sense of home in both industrial socialism and capitalism. It is not "the closed earth of the future" contrasted with "the open earth of the past." The earth has *always* been "closed," and many societies have known that. Industrial society is now discovering it daily. It is one of the strongest pressures for fundamental transformation.

COLONIZING AND ADAPTING

An analogy from biology might be helpful for understanding, from another angle, how both institutional patterns and a changing view of "creation" are pressing for metamorphosis in economic life.

In the evolution of living organisms, there are often two

distinct phases. The first is a "colonizing" phase. If it has abundant energy available, the organism exploits its environment and tends to colonize as much of its habitat as possible. It evidently has an imperialist bent and extends its own world at the growing expense of other organisms and the habitat itself. But limits are encountered, and if the organism does not want to destroy its own environs—and thus itself—it must move into an adaptive phase. Then it has its niche amid relationships of reciprocity that establish a sustainable balance.

Industrial society is still in a colonizing phase in what it treats as "an open earth." Yet the biophysical world, upon which our economic life depends, is "talking back," saying that the terms are unacceptable. Economic life in this mode is unsustainable, not only in environmental terms, but probably in political terms as well, as the great industrial systems increase an economic competition for precious resources that aggravates tensions along class, ethnic, and regional lines.

But some change of mind is occurring, and we can summarize this section with the observations of biologist Lewis Thomas:

> The oldest, easiest-to-swallow idea was that the earth was man's personal property, a combination of garden, zoo, bank vault, and energy source, placed at our disposal to be consumed, ornamented, or pulled apart as we wished.[7]

He goes on:

> In the last few years we were wrenched away from this way of looking at it. . . . It is conceded that we are not the masters of nature that we thought ourselves; we are

as dependent on the rest of life as are the leaves or midges or fish. We are part of the system.[8]

TRANSITION AND HOME AGAIN

To say that we lack historical precedents for transforming advanced industrial societies is to admit that we face economic doubt and anxiety for a long time. We are in a transition time that faces three kinds of change simultaneously. Our anxiety is real because a successful outcome is not a guarantee for any of them. *Technological change* is one imperative—and probably the easiest. Yet it is formidable because the technology needed is, for the most part, *not* the kind we know and do best—capital-intensive, energy-intensive, hyperspecialized technology reliant upon limited mineral stocks and nonrenewable energy sources. Changes in *the systems and structures* by which we organize economic life are also imperative and can involve only a range of risky experimentation as we seek to move beyond the current configurations of both industrial capitalism and industrial socialism. Not least is change needed in *our sense of home,* an altered mind-set.

These are all interconnected and add up to an arduous, probably convulsive, certainly dangerous, and likely very creative time of transition.

What should be our sense of home—to choose one arena of change addressed by Christian faith? The clue rests in an omission. In the Old Testament Hebrew vocabulary there is no word by which to separate humanity from the rest of nature. Indeed, *adam* (humanity) is of *adamah* (earth), something akin to *human* from *humus.* Or, viewing the totality of things, the Hebrew presentation is that the creation is singular, an enormously complex, ordered, and beautiful reality that is also limited and closed, circumscribed by the Creator. In this picture we are the stewards of the world, but not its masters, the priests of creation but not its engineers.

There is no place for a nature-romanticism here, that occasional Western response to industrialism and the technological order. Nature-romanticism does not understand that "the whole creation groans in travail" and, now deeply flawed, needs redemption (Rom. 8:19-23).

But there is a place for the sense of the singularity and totality of all things. This was expressed simply and movingly in 1854 by Chief Seattle. Addressing "the white man" he said:

> This we know. The earth does not belong to man; man belongs to the earth. This we know. All things are connected like the blood that unites one family. All things are connected. Whatever befalls the earth befalls the sons of the earth. Man did not weave the web of life; he is merely a strand in it. Whatever he does to the web, he does to himself . . . This earth is precious to [the Creator], and to harm the earth is to heap contempt upon its Creator.[9]

Speaking of the white man's treatment of the earth, he goes on:

> The earth is not his brother, but his enemy, and when he has conquered it, he moves on. He leaves his father's grave behind, and he does not care. He kidnaps the earth from his children. He does not care. . . . He treats his mother the earth, and his brother the sky, as things to be

> bought, plundered, sold like a sheep or
> bright beads. His appetite will devour the
> earth and leave behind only a desert.[10]

This contrasts with "the red man's" sense of home.

> Every part of this earth is sacred to my
> people. Our dead never forget this beau-
> tiful earth, for it is the mother of the red
> man. We are part of the earth and it is part
> of us. The perfumed flowers are our sis-
> ters; the deer, the horse, the great eagle,
> these are our brothers. The rocky crests,
> the juices in the meadows, the body heat
> of the pony and man—all belong to the
> same family.[11]

THE GOD-WRESTLE

If this is the mind-set which we must strive to make
our own, let us be clear that this change of mind, together with the processes of structural and technological
change, is painful. Let us also be clear that it is precisely
at the intersection of "ages" or "worlds" that Christian
faith was and is forged. Paul's call in Romans has an eery
reality: "Adapt yourselves no longer to the pattern of
this present world, but let your minds be remade and
your whole nature thus transformed (12:2 NEB). The
Greek word for mind is *nous,* referring not to the intellect
as some separate faculty, but to the whole self in its knowing. The remaking of mind means seeing things differently
and thereby having one's whole nature transformed.

The event means deep change. Jesus' word for it, and
Paul's, is *metanoia,* usually translated "repentance." It
means, literally, "a change or correction of mind." So
discipleship, which entails seeing and living the new re-

ality met in Jesus, is spoken of by Paul as "putting on the mind" of Christ Jesus. Or, alternatively, "have this mind among you, which was in Christ Jesus." That mind includes an understanding of the exercise of "dominion," something we noted in an earlier chapter.[12] And it means the cross, dying to "the pattern of this present world."

If we change the imagery somewhat, we can speak of a kind of "God-wrestle" that typifies times of transition. Indeed, this is where economic life and Christian faith now meet.

The image is from the Jacob story in Genesis 32. Jacob, on the banks of the river Jabbok, is unexpectedly seized by an unknown assailant. They struggle the night through, and Jacob, always the one in control, finds he is not. The wrestling continues until break of day when Jacob, injured, tries to wrest a blessing from the night visitor. Instead, he is given a new name. It is simultaneously a new identity. He is no longer Jacob, but Israel, one "who strove with God." Jacob comes to realize he has met more than an unknown antagonist, and he names the place Peniel, "face of God," because there he saw God "face to face."

Any time of epochal transition might be viewed as a kind of "God-wrestle." And for us, economic life in particular is now a God-wrestle: the changes entailed are both profound and painful, the future form of society is not clear, and even our very sense of "home" is at stake.

Yet the economic transformation and its turbulence is simultaneously an invitation to faith. This is what makes it a God-wrestle, the place where we might come to recognize that it is God, who in human form seizes us unexpectedly in the events and challenges of economic life, many of which we would not have chosen—even though we did much to create them. And like Jacob, it is with God we struggle through a long night, "until break of day."

Pain and injury occur. Yet, only here, in the God-wrestle, does transformation take place. Only here is the antagonist recognized as the one in whom God is encountered.[13]

Faith is forged in such transformation. It knows the dynamic of dying and rising as the most profound dynamic of everyday life. This is why, at its own deepest levels, economic anxiety and the conditions that make for it are also an invitation to faith. In the remembering of the creative event of the past and in the straining forward we call hope, we meet the transforming God who "summons things that are not yet in existence as if they already were" (Rom. 4:17 NEB).

notes

1. Economic Anxiety and Doubt

1. W. Michael Blumenthal, "Remarks Before the New York Financial Writers Association," New York City, June 7, 1979, p. 1. Available from The Department of the Treasury, Washington, D.C.
2. Quoted in Walter Wink in "Unmasking the Powers," *Sojourners*, October 1978, p. 9.
3. Quoted from Ellen Goodman in "On Women's Issues, Schizophrenia," *The Washington Post*, November 15, 1979.
4. Reported by Amitai Etzioni, in "The Inflation Habit: A Case of Stunted Growth," *Psychology Today*, May 1979, p. 14.
5. *Time* essay, June 4, 1979, p. 55.
6. Michael Korda, "Hooray for Hedonism," *Newsweek*, November 26, 1979, p. 29.
7. Blumenthal, p. 2.
8. *Ibid.*
9. *Ibid.*
10. *Ibid.*
11. *Ibid.*
12. *Ibid.*
13. Alfred Kahn, quoted in "U.S. Reports Fresh Signs of Recession," *The Washington Post*, May 1, 1980.
14. Blumenthal, p. 2.
15. Reported by Etzioni, p. 14.
16. Ellen Goodman, "That Something Called Progress," *The Washington Post*, July 24, 1979.

116

2. Economics, Ethics, and Religion

1. *Luther's Large Catechism,* Augsburg, 1935, p. 44.
2. Luther, p. 45.
3. A helpful discussion of the relation of ethics to economics is found in J. Philip Wogaman, *The Great Economic Debate: An Ethical Analysis,* Westminster, 1977, pp. 1-10. Some of the questions in this paragraph are taken from his discussion.
4. The list of assumptions is adapted from Bruce C. Birch and Larry L. Rasmussen, *The Predicament of the Prosperous,* Westminster, 1978, pp. 44-45.

3. Interplay of Faith and Economic Values

1. Quoted in Sydney E. Ahlstrom, *A Religious History of the American People,* Yale University Press, 1972, pp. 789-790.
2. Quoted in Ahlstrom, p. 789.
3. Noted in Max Weber, *The Protestant Ethic and the Spirit of Capitalism,* transl. by Talcott Parsons, Charles Scribner's Sons, 1958, p. 175.
4. *Ibid.*
5. *Ibid.*
6. Langdon Gilkey, *Shantung Compound.* Harper and Row, copyright 1966, p. 228.

4. Interplay of Economic Values and Culture

1. The term "Economic Man" is a use of "man" more inclusive than "man" may connote. I am not altering it to be more clearly generic, however, because the reality pointed to by "Economic Man" has, in fact, been overwhelmingly masculine.
2. Carl Sandburg, "Chicago." The full text is included in the Study Project at the conclusion of this chapter. From *Complete Poems,* Harcourt, Brace & World, 1950.
3. Ronald H. Preston, *Religion and the Persistence of Capitalism,* SCM Press, 1979, p. 35.
4. *Ibid.*
5. Daniel Bell, *The Cultural Contradictions of Capitalism,* Basic Books, Inc., Publishers, 1976, pp. 13-14.

6. Taken, with slight changes to correct sexist language, from Preston, pp. 73-74.
7. From a flyer in the student center at The American University, Washington, D.C.
8. *Ibid.*
9. Quotations are from James T. Yenckel's interview with Robert C. Weigl, "Private Lives: The Portable Self," in the *Washington Post,* April 9, 1980.
10. From T. S. Eliot, "Choruses from 'The Rock,'" in *Collected Poems:* 1909-1962, Harcourt Brace Jovanovich, Inc., 1963.
11. Bell, pp. 13-14.
12. Bruce C. Birch and Larry L. Rasmussen, *The Predicament of the Prosperous,* Westminster Press, 1978, p. 21.
13. A 1979 ad by The Hearst Corporation for *Cosmopolitan* magazine.

5. Capitalisms and Socialisms

1. J. Philip Wogaman, *The Great Economic Debate: An Ethical Analysis,* Westminster, 1977, "Contents."
2. Michael Harrington, *The Vast Majority: A Journey to the World's Poor,* Simon and Schuster, 1977, p. 227.
3. George Dalton, *Economic Systems and Society,* Penguin Books, 1974, p. 47.
4. Dalton, p. 179.
5. Dalton, pp. 179-180.
6. Reinhold Niebuhr, *The Irony of American History,* Charles Scribner's Sons, 1962, p. 30.
7. Wogaman, pp. 51-53.

6. Rich and Poor

1. From *Focus,* publication of the Office for Governmental Affairs, Lutheran Council in the USA, Vol. 13, No. 5, May 1979, p. 1.
2. Walter Buehlmann, *The Coming of the Third Church,* New York, 1976, p. 20.
3. Buehlmann, p. 58, and 1978 *Atlas,* The World Bank, Washington, D.C.
4. *Ibid.*
5. Buehlmann, p. 58.

6. Michael Harrington, *The Vast Majority: A Journey to the World's Poor*, New York, 1977, p. 235.
7. From *Focus*, p. 1.

7. Grave Doubts About Growth

1. Herman E. Daly, *Steady-State Economics*, W. H. Freeman and Co., 1977, p. 99.
2. See Fred Hirsch, *Social Limits to Growth*, Harvard University Press, 1976.
3. Charles West, "Justice Within the Limits of the Created World," *Ecumenical Review*, Vol. XXVII, No. 1 (January 1975), p. 57.
4. Reinhold Niebuhr, *The Irony of American History*, Charles Scribner's Sons, 1962, pp. 56-57.

8. Gaining a Christian Perspective

1. The title of a subsection in Herman Daly's *Steady-State Economics*, p. 99.
2. Daly, *Steady-State Economics*, p. 45.
3. Philip Slater, *The Pursuit of Loneliness: American Culture at the Breaking Point*, Beacon Press, 1970, p. 7.
4. H. Richard Niebuhr and others, *The Purpose of the Church and Its Ministry: Reflections on the Aims of Theological Education*, Harper and Row, 1956, p. 38.
5. Douglas John Hall, *Lighten Our Darkness*, Westminster, 1976, p. 80ff.
6. Kingsley Davis, "Sociological Aspects of Genetic Control," in *Readings in Population*, edited by William Petersen, Macmillan, 1972, p. 379.
7. J. Philip Wogaman, *The Great Economic Debate*, p. 53.
8. See the discussion in Wogaman, *The Great Economic Debate*, chap. 3, "Moral Foundations," especially pp. 51-53.
9. Quoted by Erik H. Erikson in *Gandhi's Truth: On the Origins of Militant Non-Violence*, p. 281.
10. Francine Cardman, sermon preached in Oxnam Chapel, Wesley Theological Seminary, Washington, D.C., October 7, 1977.
11. Gustave Martelet, *The Risen Christ and the Eucharistic World*, Seabury, 1976, p. 183.

9. The Church in the 1980s

1. Douglas John Hall, *Lighten Our Darkness: Toward an Indigenous Theology of the Cross*, Westminster, 1976, pp. 43ff.
2. See Bruce C. Birch and Larry L. Rasmussen, *The Predicament of the Prosperous*, Westminster, 1978, pp. 186-194, "What Form for the Church?" The images of the church in this chapter draw heavily from that earlier writing.
3. Hall, pp. 73ff.
4. The image is that of Rubem Alves in *Tomorrow's Child*, Harper & Row, 1972, p. 204.
5. The phrase is taken from an article by David Dodson Gray, "Good-bye More—Hello Less," in *JSAC Grapevine*, Vol. 11, No. 6, January 1980.
6. The title of John V. Taylor's book, *Enough Is Enough*, Augsburg Publishing House, 1977.
7. "A Fable for Now: Why Elephants Can't Live on Peanuts," available from the Mobil Corporation.
8. Paul grounds this economic advice theologically in the incarnation, life, and death of Jesus Christ. See 2 Corinthians 8:1-15.
9. G. K. Chesterton, *The Man Who Was Thursday*, G. P. Putnam's Sons, 1960, pp. 9-10.
10. Alexander Schmemann, *For the Life of the World: Sacraments and Orthodoxy*, St. Vladimir's Seminary Press, 1973, p. 11. The sexist language in this quotation, as well as in many others in this book, gives cause for a brief comment. I have left direct quotations uncorrected. For the remaining materials, including paraphrased remarks, I have sought to avoid sexist terms.
11. See Howard Becker, "Processes of Secularization: An Ideal-Typical Analysis with Special Reference to Personality Change as Affected by Population Movement," *The Sociological Review*, Vol. XXIV, 1932, pp. 138-154, 266-286.
12. R. H. Tawney, *Religion and the Rise of Capitalism*, Harcourt, Brace and World, Inc., 1926, p. 235.
13. See Walter Brueggemann, *The Prophetic Imagination*, Fortress Press, 1978.
14. The phrase is David Riesman's, from "Some Observations on Community Plans and Utopia," in his *Individualism Reconsidered and Other Essays*, Free Press, 1954, p. 70. Riesman's reference is not to the church, however.

15. *Ibid.*
16. Reinhold Niebuhr, *The Irony of American History*, Charles Scribner's Sons, 1962, p. 63.
17. This paragraph is based on the closing of the book by Alves, *Tomorrow's Child.*

10. The God-Wrestle

1. See the discussion at the outset of Chapter 6.
2. Matthew Fox, *A Spirituality Named Compassion* (Minneapolis: Winston Press, 1979), p. 177. The entire chapter, "Economics and Compassion," is pertinent to our subject.
3. Dietrich Bonhoeffer, *Letters and Papers from Prison* (New York: The Macmillan Company, 1972), p. 380.
4. The phrase is from the title of a book by Joseph C. Pearce, *The Crack in the Cosmic Egg: Challenging Constructs of Mind and Reality* (New York: Simon and Schuster, 1973).
5. See the epigraph to Chapter 7.
6. Kenneth E. Boulding, "The Economics of the Coming Spaceship Earth," in Herman E. Daly, ed., *Toward a Steady-State Economy* (San Francisco: W. H. Freeman & Co., 1973), pp. 122, 127. Cited by Matthew Fox in *A Spirituality Named Compassion*, p. 281.
7. Lewis Thomas, *The Lives of a Cell* (New York: Bantam Books, 1975), p. 122. Cited by Fox, p. 185.
8. *Ibid.*
9. From "The Decidedly Unforked Message of Chief Seattle," in *Passages*, April, 1974, p. 19.
10. *Ibid.*
11. *Ibid.*
12. See the discussion in Chapter 8 above.
13. See the use of this story and the discussion preceding it in Birch and Rasmussen, *The Predicament of the Prosperous* (Philadelphia: Westminster Press, 1978), pp. 74-75. The use here paraphrases that earlier writing.

for further study

Birch, Bruce C. and Larry L. Rasmussen, *The Predicament of the Prosperous*. Westminster, 1978. Some of the study materials come from this book, especially those for Chapter 2. The book can profitably be consulted for other materials, including major essays on relevant biblical materials and essays offering a constructive theological position for American Christians today.

Hall, Douglas John. *Lighten Our Darkness: Toward an Indigenous Theology of the Cross*. Westminster, 1976. Difficult but important treatment of North American culture and a constructive theological response to its failures. Particular insight is drawn from Luther's theology of the cross.

Harrington, Michael. *The Vast Majority: A Journey to the World's Poor*. Simon and Schuster, 1977. An American's travels in several low-income countries, with reflections on the relationships and structures that maintain global wealth and poverty.

Heilbroner, Robert. *An Inquiry Into the Human Prospect*. W. W. Norton, 1974. An economist and social philosopher conducts a penetrating analysis of modern industrial society and speculates about the future in answer to his overarching question, "Is there hope for humankind?"

Hellwig, Monica. *The Eucharist and the Hunger of the World.* Paulist, 1976. Connects the spiritual impulse with the concrete, physical needs of the planet's population, seeing the central action of Holy Communion as the sharing of food. A popular treatment of Christian mission in a hungry world.

Niebuhr, Reinhold. *The Irony of American History.* Charles Scribner's Sons, 1962. The chapter, "Prosperity and Virtue," is a brilliant analysis of the relationship of happiness, economic prosperity, and moral virtue in American life and thought.

Sider, Ronald J. *Rich Christians in an Age of Hunger.* Paulist, 1977. Richly biblical study of relationships between the prosperous and the poor, by a conservative evangelical scholar. Includes creative ideas on Christian sharing, including a "graduated tithe" for the comfortable Christian seeking to live at a responsible level of consumption.

Stivers, Robert. *The Sustainable Society: Ethics and Economic Growth.* Westminster, 1976. A teacher of Christian ethics at Pacific Lutheran University surveys the "limits to growth" debate and offers his critique.

Taylor, John V. *Enough Is Enough.* Augsburg, 1977. Deservedly popular treatment of consumerist society by a British bishop. Especially useful is its chapter on "A Theology of Enough." Complete with study guide, the book is ideally suited for group discussion.

Taylor, Richard K. *Economics and the Gospel.* United Church Press, 1973. A popular statement of biblical perspectives on economic justice. Includes discussion questions.

Wogaman, J. Philip. *The Great Economic Debate: An Ethical Analysis*. Westminster, 1977. Ethical grounds for evaluating economic systems in light of the Judeo-Christian theological tradition. Reviews five economic types: laissez-faire capitalism, Marxism, democratic socialism, social market (mixed economy) capitalism, and economic conservationism.